Past Masters

General Editor   Keith Thomas

Rousseau

Robert Wokler is Reader in the History of Political Thought in the Department of Government at the University of Manchester. His books include *Rousseau on Society, Politics, Music and Language* (New York, 1987) and *Rousseau's Enlightenment* (Cambridge, forthcoming), and he is joint editor of *Diderot's Political Writings* (Cambridge, 1992), John Plamenatz's *Man and Society* (London, expanded and revised edition, 1992), *Rousseau and The Eighteenth Century* (Oxford, 1992), and *The Cambridge History of Eighteenth-Century Political Thought* (Cambridge, forthcoming).

Past Masters

Robert Wokler

Rousseau

Oxford New York

OXFORD UNIVERSITY PRESS

1995

Oxford University Press, Walton Street, Oxford OX2 6DP

Oxford New York
Athens Auckland Bangkok Bombay
Calcutta Cape Town Dar es Salaam Delhi
Florence Hong Kong Istanbul Karachi
Kuala Lumpur Madras Madrid Melbourne
Mexico City Nairobi Paris Singapore
Taipei Tokyo Toronto
and associated companies in
Berlin Ibadan

Oxford is a trade mark of Oxford University Press

First published 1995 as an Oxford University Press paperback

British Library Cataloguing in Publication Data
Data available

Library of Congress Cataloging in Publication Data
Wokler, Robert, 1942–
    Rousseau / Robert Wokler.
      p.   cm.
    Includes index.
    1. Rousseau, Jean-Jacques, 1712–1778—Criticism and
interpretation.   I. Title.
PQ2053.W64   1995   848'.509—dc20   94–18360
    ISBN 0–19–287640–6

10 9 8 7 6 5 4 3 2 1

Typeset by Graphicraft Typesetters Ltd., Hong Kong
Printed in Great Britain
by Biddles Ltd.
Guildford & King's Lynn

For Isaiah Berlin

Acknowledgements

This work required not very much longer to complete than the eight weeks originally anticipated, but those weeks were assembled over a period of not much less than eight years. I have adapted a few pages from earlier publications, as follows: from 'Rousseau', in *Political Thought from Plato to Nato* (London, 1984), in Chapter 1; from 'The *Discours sur les sciences et les arts* and its Offspring', in *Reappraisals of Rousseau*, ed. S. Harvey, M. Hobson, *et al.* (Manchester, 1980), and 'Rousseau on Rameau and Revolution', in *Studies in the Eighteenth Century*, vol. iv, ed. R. F. Brissenden and J. C. Eade (Canberra, 1979), in Chapter 2; and from 'Rousseau's Two Concepts of Liberty' in *Lives, Liberties and the Public Good*, ed. G. Feaver and F. Rosen (London, 1987), in Chapter 4. Wherever possible, I have tried to incorporate corrections or improvements kindly drawn to my notice by John Hope Mason and Quentin Skinner. For his unimaginably patient forbearance in permitting me to attend to other publishing crises as they arose, and for his meticulous refinements of my style, I am indebted to Sir Keith Thomas. For their unstinting encouragement beyond all reasonable call of duty, my thanks are also due to my editors, Susie Casement and Catherine Clarke, at the Oxford University Press. For preparing a presentable typescript in the format required, I am grateful to Marilyn Dunn and Karen Hall.

November 1993

Contents

Abbreviations

A   *Politics and the Arts: Letter to M. d'Alembert on the Theatre* by J.-J. Rousseau, trans. with notes and an introduction by Allan Bloom (Ithaca, NY: Cornell University Press, 1977) (first published in this format in 1960)

C   Rousseau, *The Confessions*, trans. and with an introduction by J. M. Cohen (London: Penguin Books, 1953)

E   Rousseau, *Emile, or On Education*, introduction, trans., and notes by Allan Bloom (New York: Basic Books, 1979)

G   Rousseau, *The First and Second Discourses, together with the Replies to Critics and Essay on the Origin of Languages*, ed., trans., and annotated by Victor Gourevitch (New York: Harper Row, Perennial Library, 1986)

H   *Rousseau on International Relations*, ed. Stanley Hoffmann and David Fidler (Oxford: Clarendon Press, 1991)

L   Rousseau, *Correspondance complète*, ed. and annotated by R. A. Leigh (Geneva and Oxford: The Voltaire Foundation, 1965–)

P   Rousseau, *Œuvres complètes*, ed. B. Gagnebin, M. Raymond, *et al.* (Paris: Gallimard, Bibliothèque de la Pléiade, 1959–)

R   Rousseau, *Reveries of the Solitary Walker*, trans. with an introduction by Peter France (London: Penguin Books, 1979)

Only the most accessible (some even abbreviated) English editions of Rousseau's works are cited, and I have often preferred my own translation while nevertheless pointing to the location of another. For writings not yet available in the Pléiade edition of his *Œuvres complètes*, I refer exclusively to the best English translation, where there is one. All references to the *Social Contract* are to its internal books and chapters only. All references to the *Correspondance complète* are to a letter number.

1 The Life and Times of a Citizen of Geneva

Together with Montesquieu, Hume, Smith, and Kant among his contemporaries, Rousseau has exerted the most profound influence on modern European intellectual history, perhaps even surpassing anyone else of his day. No other eighteenth-century thinker contributed more major writings in so wide a range of subjects and forms, nor wrote with such sustained passion and eloquence. No one else managed through both his works and his life to excite or disturb public imagination so deeply. Almost alone among the seminal figures of the Enlightenment, he subjected the main currents of the world he inhabited to the most inspired censure, even while channelling their direction, and when French Revolutionary leaders later seized their opportunity to ignite the unity of political practice and theory, it was to his doctrines above all that they professed their allegiance.

Like most distinguished men in his world's republic of letters, Rousseau of course had many interests apart from politics. He was a much-admired composer and the author of a substantial and learned dictionary of music, a subject which perhaps claimed more of his attention throughout his life than any other. While a number of his most important early writings dealt with the arts and sciences and the philosophy of history, the main enthusiasm of his later years proved to be botany, to which he devoted a collection of letters that in translation was to prove a popular textbook in England. His *Reveries of the Solitary Walker* were to spark an explosion of Romantic naturalism throughout Europe in the late eighteenth century, while his *New Héloïse* was the most widely read novel of his age. His *Confessions*, moreover, comprise the most important work of autobiography since that of St Augustine, and his *Émile* the most significant work on education after Plato's *Republic*. Yet it is as a moralist and political thinker that he achieved his greatest distinction.

His birthplace and early childhood were to leave deep impressions upon his life and the development of his thought. He was born in 1712, in Geneva, a small Calvinist country surrounded by large, predominantly Catholic, nations; a mountainous state protected from invasion by natural barriers and the political culture of its citizens; above all, a republic in the midst of duchies and monarchies. When Rousseau would later describe the Savoyard vicar of *Émile* as professing his faith to a benign god of Nature rather than Scriptures, on a hill overlooking a city, he conceived an image of man's direct communion with his maker such as could be shared by few of the inhabitants of the other cities he knew. In their opposition to arbitrary government and the privileges of a venal aristocracy, many of the *philosophes* of the eighteenth century regarded progressive monarchs as allies in the cause of reform. Rousseau, however, showed none of the confidence of his contemporaries in the prospects of enlightened absolutism. Where a radical commitment, tempered by fear of censorship, inspired Diderot, Voltaire, and others to publish their writings anonymously, he took every opportunity to sign his works 'Citizen of Geneva', and ceased to do so only after he was convinced that his compatriots had irredeemably lost their way. No other figure of the Enlightenment was more hostile to the course that political civilization had taken and at the same time so proud of his political identity.

Rousseau's mother died just after giving birth to him, and responsibility for his upbringing thus fell to his father, a watchmaker of romantic and irascible temperament, who inspired in him a love of Nature and books, especially the classics and history. He never received a formal education, and he occasionally appeared to compensate for that deficiency by annotating his writings with lengthy footnotes which acknowledged sources that his better-schooled contemporaries scarcely troubled to cite. But his mother had inherited a large library, and his well-read father encouraged his own fascination with literature, in a cultivated manner which Rousseau in his *Confessions* found distinctive of Genevan artisans by contrast with those of other countries. It was from his father that he also inherited much of his zealous devotion to his birthplace, where, as he would be told, 'all men are brothers', and 'joy and heaven reign'. At least two of his principal works, the *Letter to d'Alembert on the Theatre* of 1758 and his

Letters from the Mountain of 1764, were to be devoted mainly to the culture or political system of his native city, and he was to remark that his *Social Contract* itself had been designed to portray the noble principles of that state. Nowhere in his writings is his conception of political fraternity more richly drawn than in his *Letter to d'Alembert*, when he recalls the convivial celebrations in the open air of a Genevan military regiment which had fired his imagination as a young boy (A 135–6 n.).

His attachment to his father and to the city of his birth did not, however, overcome the loss of his mother. When only fifteen, he was introduced to a Swiss baroness, Madame de Warens, who lived at Annecy in the Duchy of Savoy, just west of Geneva. Madame de Warens had by the still tender age of twenty-nine already made something of a career of converting Protestant refugees to Catholicism, and she brought Rousseau into her home and her bosom with an intimate hospitality that accorded well with his own rapturous enthusiasm. For the next ten years, first at Annecy and then Chambéry and finally in the idyllic retreat of the valley of Les Charmettes, he was to become both her lover and pupil. With her guidance and some assistance from her own patrons and religious confessors, he completed his education, especially in philosophy and modern literature, of which he had had little knowledge before, and began to contemplate a career as a writer. Partly inspired by Madame de Warens' pietist enthusiasms, furthermore, Rousseau formed an attachment to the Deity and to the marvels of His Creation which was to distinguish his religious beliefs from those of most of his contemporaries among the *philosophes*, who were either atheists or sceptics and suspicious of his zealotry, regarding it as akin to the mystical superstitions of a clerical Church that they aimed to bring down. Throughout their time as lovers, and for the rest of his life, Rousseau was to call Madame de Warens his *maman*, ascribing to her those qualities of sweetness, grace, and beauty which, as a motherless child, he longed to find in all the women under whose spell he was later to fall.

Thérèse Levasseur, with whom he lived from about 1745 until his death, and whom he was eventually to marry, was a somewhat less attractive and far less educated woman, who despite her originally compelling unspoilt freshness never came to command his affections in the same way. Rather in need of maternal care as well as sexual gratification from both of the leading women in his life, he could never tolerate a family of his own, and he abandoned the five children he had by Thérèse to the uncertain fate of a public orphanage. Rousseau would later claim that he had been too impoverished to care for his children properly, but his own conduct towards them filled him with remorse and shame. It certainly made readers wonder how he could write so sublime a treatise on the education of children as *Émile*, which may in some respects be read as a work of personal atonement. To this day, his abandonment of his children has coloured the popular image of his character far more than any of his other traits.

He was also to prove less solicitous than he might have been of the needs of Madame de Warens, when in the 1750s she fell into a condition of extreme financial hardship and was even forced to register as a pauper. She was to die, with no relief from her poverty, and no contact with Rousseau, in the summer of 1762, when he was absorbed with anxieties for his own safety, following the denunciation of his writings by religious or secular authorities in both France and Switzerland. On Palm Sunday, or 12 April, 1778, a few weeks away from death himself, he penned one of his most eloquent pages, the Tenth Walk of his *Reveries*, where he reflects that it was then fifty years to the day since he had first met Madame de Warens, with whom his destiny had been intertwined and in whose arms he had enjoyed a brief and tender period of his life in which he had been utterly himself, 'without obstacle or mixed emotion and when [he] could truly say that [he] had lived' (P i. 1098–9, R 153).

When in his late twenties Rousseau finally began to make his independent way in the world, he earned a modest livelihood mainly from private tuition and from the transcription of music, resolving to conquer Paris with a comic play, *Narcissus*, and a new system of musical notation. Soon after his arrival there in 1741 he was befriended by Diderot, who was of similar age, background, and ambition and was to become his most intimate companion over the next fifteen years. The two men did not really possess the same temperament, with Diderot rather more urbane and affable, and Rousseau more sensitive and earnest, but they shared common interests in the theatre, the sciences, and especially music.

On Diderot's apppointment with d'Alembert as joint editors of the *Encyclopédie*, Rousseau was commissioned to write most of the articles on musical subjects and another on political economy. In 1749, following the publication of his *Letter on the Blind*, Diderot suffered a brief period of detention in the prison of Vincennes, and Rousseau came to see him almost daily, imploring the authorities to release his companion. It was on his way there one day from his lodgings in Paris that he came across the notice of a prize essay competition on the subject of the arts and sciences and their moral impact on mankind, which was to alter the course of his life. Diderot at first shared Rousseau's enthusiasm for the argument against civilization that forms the first *Discourse,* but only because he warmed to the provocative idea that a principal contributor to his dictionary of the arts and sciences should also undertake to discredit them. He was later to espouse radical moral ideas of his own, some of which were to bear a striking resemblance to those of Rousseau himself, although he always remained convinced of what Rousseau had denied—that the progress of knowledge and culture leads to the improvement of human conduct and behaviour, whenever it springs from such genuine curiosity as is compatible with man's nature.

Rousseau's stay in Paris had been interrupted briefly by his appointment in 1743–4 as Secretary to the French Ambassador in Venice. As a youth he had already visited Turin and learnt Italian there, relishing Italian music, which he heard frequently, with an ardent enthusiasm for its spontaneity and directness that would never be tempered by any similar appreciation of the refinement of French musical textures. In Turin he had found the splendid orchestral performances which accompanied the liturgy of the mass more appealing than the austere psalms that passed for music in the churches of Geneva, and in Venice he enthused as well over secular and vernacular music, which suffused his senses with popular tunes drawn from the streets and taverns no less than from the stage. Later, on his return to Paris, he was to contrast Italian opera favourably with that of France, on the grounds that the French language was less amenable to musical expression and that the French style of vocal music characteristically lacked a clear melodic line and was too much encumbered by superficial ornamentation and harmonic embellishments.

His mid-century quarrel with Rameau, France's leading composer and musical theorist of the day, was to turn on just such themes, and his *Letter on French Music* of 1753, for which he was to be hanged in effigy because its reflections on music were thought seditious, was to prove one of his most combustible works, and the only one which, as he claims in his *Confessions* (P i. 384, C 358), ever put a halt to a political uprising in France. The monarchy's expulsion of the magistrates of the Paris *Parlement* in November of that year, in a national crisis which also turned upon the conflict between Jansenists and Jesuits, had caused great turmoil, but not, he maintains, so much as had been stirred by his work on music, which had averted a potential revolution against the state by turning it into a revolution against him. Paradoxically, the *Letter on French Music* proved to be his sole composition to win the almost universal endorsement of the *philosophes*, who took up the cause of Italian music with scarcely less enthusiasm. In 1752 Rousseau composed an opera, *Le Devin du village* or *Village Soothsayer*, which he produced in the Italian style and which came to be admired and even imitated, as well as surpassed in quality, by Gluck and Mozart. When he published his *Dictionary of Music* in 1767, largely developed from his articles for the *Encyclopédie*, he was to pursue his earlier ideas on music and opera in more detail than ever before, while in the *Essay on the Origin of Languages*, dating mainly from the early 1760s, he managed to join those ideas with his philosophy of history, ascribing greater musical vitality to classical Latin over contemporary French, and more virtue and liberty to the citizens of ancient republics, who had, he suggests, expressed their fraternal feelings in open-textured song of a kind no longer prevalent among the modern subjects of monarchical rule.

In his *Confessions* Rousseau remarks on his having also discovered, in Venice, that 'Everything depends entirely upon politics', and that therefore 'a people is everywhere nothing but what its government makes of it' (P i. 404, C 377). Mankind was not naturally evil, he was convinced, but all too frequently became so under poor governments which generated vice. If everything depends upon politics then the upright character of his Genevan compatriots, on the one hand, and the moral corruption of a once-illustrious Venetian Republic, on the other, could both be traced to a similar source. Following his stay in Venice and his return to Paris, the capital of the greatest monarchy of the day, Rousseau was thus in a position to compare the contributions of three very distinct regimes, each having responsibility for shaping the character of its people. His first opportunity to draw together his ideas about the decline of culture and the political roots of vice arose in 1749, when he drafted his *Discourse on the Arts and Sciences*. While our forebears had been robust, the excess of luxury upon which enlightenment feeds has sapped us of our vitality and made us slaves to the trappings of culture, he contends there. Sparta had formed a durable nation so long as it was unadorned by the arts and sciences, but Athens, the most civilized state of antiquity, had been unable to arrest its decay into despotism, and the increasing grandeur of Rome and other empires had been accompanied by the decline of their military and political strength. Everywhere, Rousseau remarks, 'the arts, letters, and sciences are spread like garlands of flowers round the iron chains by which [men] are weighed down' (P iii. 7, G 4–5).

This first of his two *Discourses* won the literary prize for which he entered it, and almost overnight the fuss it excited transformed him from an obscure man of letters approaching his middle age to the most celebrated scourge of modern civilization. One of the main factors underlying its notoriety was its manner of reversing a stock-in-trade eighteenth-century perspective of the epic struggle between virtue and vice. Voltaire spoke on behalf of many men of enlightened opinion in his day when, in his *Philosophical Letters* and elsewhere, he joined virtue to the advancement of learning and science and portrayed the progressive improvement of human conduct in the light of modern Europe's slow awakening from dark centuries of superstition and ignorance. Diderot and d'Alembert had conceived their *Encyclopédie* along much the same lines. Rousseau, by contrast, appeared to extol the merits of a barbarous golden age, from which mankind had fallen and lost grace because of an idolatrous lust for learning. Not only did he thus give the impression of favouring savagery over culture; to his enlightened contemporaries he seemed also to have forgotten that the principal source of misery and despair in the contemporary world, the Christian Church, drew its power from much the same mysticism reinforced by ignorance which in the ancient world he applauded. Voltaire and his followers denounced this vision of our uncultivated innocence, and they accused Rousseau of having abandoned the causes of political and religious reform to which he should have been allied so that he might instead return to a primitive state of uncouth stupidity. That assessment of his theory of man's nature was in many ways wide of the mark, but it did place due weight upon one of the central tenets of his philosophy—which he often avowed to be the guiding thread of his works—that while our Creator had made everything good, all that had been forged by man was corrupt and depraved. Evil, Rousseau believed, was the characteristic outcome of human enterprise, if not always the object of human design.

In the early 1750s he was absorbed mainly with his writings on music and with meeting the objections of some of the critics of his *Discourse on the Arts and Sciences*. To those who directed his attention away from the depravity of culture and towards the pernicious influence of political and economic factors instead, he owed a certain debt, since they reiterated the truth, as he saw it, of his Venetian discovery. By the autumn of 1753 he was to embark on a new and more subtle version of his philosophy of history, in which the pursuit of inequality rather than that of luxury would be held responsible for our moral corruption, and in which he would take the relations of authority built round the institution of private property as the principal cause of humanity's decline. The publicly authorized appropriation of the earth by some men at the expense of others must have led to the establishment of civil society through guile and injustice, Rousseau contends in his *Discourse on Inequality* of 1755, where he pursues that thesis in terms of a conjectural history of the human race, in which he also attempts to explain the social genesis of the family and of agriculture, and depicts the origins of different types of government in terms of the unequal distributions of private property that must have underpinned them.

In this hypothetical reconstruction of the past, he makes several observations of importance to his political and social theory which he had not articulated before. His fresh emphasis upon the institution of private property, rather than the pursuit of culture and learning, as the main source of our moral corruption was designed to challenge what Rousseau had come to understand as the foundations of modern jurisprudence from Grotius and Hobbes to Pufendorf and Locke. No other thinker of the Enlightenment was to challenge that tradition so directly as Rousseau in his second *Discourse*, and no other eighteenth-century critique of earlier views of human nature was to offer such a dramatic conception of the evolutionary metamorphosis of our societal traits. Rousseau's abstraction of primitive from civilized man in this work, moreover, came to be drawn around a dichotomy between our physical and moral attributes which he had not previously addressed. Morality, he now insisted, did not stem from human nature but rather from the denaturation of man in society, with the striking inequalities that shaped our lives utterly different in kind from the insignificant natural variations between us. So far from expressing the best of what was latent in human nature, the establishment of private property, he argues in the *Discourse on Inequality*, had deformed it, turning the pursuit of honour and public esteem into an ignoble and dispiriting kind of competition. The hypothetical portrait of our original traits which he offers here for the first time actually drew savage man closer to other animals than to civilized man, giving Rousseau scope to speculate on zoological themes and on our differences from apes and other primates. Mankind, he had come to believe, was for better or worse the only species in Nature which could make its own history, and the abuse of our capacities had ensured that in society we lived more anxious and miserable lives than all other creatures.

The second *Discourse* was in time to exercise a profound influence upon the development of European thought in a variety of disciplines, but initially it had a less dramatic impact on its readers than his *Discourse on the Arts and Sciences* or his *Letter on French Music*. For the *philosophes* with whom he had been previously allied, however, it confirmed and compounded their fears that his first *Discourse* was a statement of genuine belief and that he could no longer be regarded as an ally of enlightenment or progress. The need for him to part company with some of his former friends had certainly become apparent to Rousseau himself, who had always felt unease among atheists and sceptics. His unfashionable zeal, masked only by a certain timidity in public, had no doubt been inspired partly by Madame de Warens, and, in

9

turn, it struck some of his Parisian friends, eventually Diderot himself, as evidence of insufferable self-righteousness and vanity.

When he began to quarrel with his companions in the mid-1750s, he claimed that he could no longer tolerate their moral complacency. At first he planned to return to Geneva, and was dissuaded from that move mainly by Voltaire's decision to settle there himself. Already twice imprisoned in the Bastille, Voltaire had merely sought a haven from which he might pursue his interests with less risk to his safety and in a milieu more congenial than the world of King Frederick the Great of Prussia, where bayonets had been preferred to books; but Rousseau perceived sinister motives in this encroachment of his native city. Voltaire would transform the simple manners of his compatriots into those of corrupt Parisians, he feared, so that in returning to his birthplace he would confront the same vices as had made him flee from France. He therefore decided instead to accept a country retreat called *The Hermitage*, just north of Paris in the forest of Montmorency, offered to him by a friend of Diderot, Madame d'Épinay, who for a brief period was his benefactress and closest confidante, though she later proved the fiercest of all his adversaries who had known him well. With his arrival on 9 April 1756 began his disengagement from nearly all the *philosophes* with whom he had been allied since the early 1740s. He was soon to quarrel with Diderot, who had written a play in this period, *The Natural Son*, dealing in part with the evils of solitude, which he read as a personal gesture of contempt. When in 1756 Voltaire produced his poems on Natural Law and on the Lisbon earthquake of the previous year, in which he mocked the folly of blind faith in Providence that all was as it should be, Rousseau replied with his so-called 'Letter on Providence' that God was not responsible for evil and that the world of human suffering of which Voltaire complained had been manufactured only by man. Voltaire's sarcastic response to Rousseau (as well as to Leibniz and Pope) was to take the form of a moral tale, which he entitled *Candide*.

By 1758 Rousseau had effectively come to break off all relations with his former associates. A year earlier d'Alembert had produced a substantial article on Geneva for volume vii of the *Encyclopédie*, in which he put the case for the establishment of a theatre in that city, which would enhance its culture, and thereby promote the moral sophistication of its citizens as well. Rousseau was convinced that Voltaire had conspired with d'Alembert in writing this essay, and he conceived his *Letter to d'Alembert on the Theatre* as much to refute that usurper of his birthright as to confront d'Alembert himself. He decried the art of stagecraft as unsuited to the spirit of fraternal love which had once prevailed, and was now in need of restoration, in his native city. Just as Plato had chosen to expel the captivating but factitious beauties of Homeric myth from his virtuous Republic, so Rousseau, in his *Letter to d'Alembert*, attempted to preserve Geneva from the all too subtle irony of Molière, who could wonderfully transform pious integrity into hypocritical mischief, through entertainments of gnarled subterfuge and veiled exchanges which, in confining his compatriots as rapt spectators of devious intent, would thereby sap the nation of the transparent ardour of its own strength.

It was also in the period immediately following his flight from Paris that Rousseau drafted his *Julie, or The New Héloïse*, the most popular work of fiction in late eighteenth-century France. This epistolary tale about the tribulations of frustrated love in its conflict with duty was partly inspired by the novels of Richardson and Prévost, and it contains some of Rousseau's most lyrical passages on romantic affection, tender sexuality, and rustic simplicity. If *Candide* was, in part, Voltaire's fictional response to his 'Letter on Providence', then the preface to the *New Héloïse* may be regarded as the postscript to the *Letter to d'Alembert* which Rousseau had really meant to address to Voltaire. 'Theatre is required in great cities', Rousseau writes, 'and a corrupt people needs its novels. I have witnessed the manners of the day and have published these letters. If only I could have lived in a century when I should have been obliged to throw them away!' (P ii. 5).

In the same period, Rousseau completed his *Émile*, a work of almost equal length to *The New Héloïse*, and which bears some relation to it, not least because it also concludes as a novel, although it begins as a treatise on education. The first book of the text opens with the statement of a principle which Rousseau had come by the mid-1750s to regard as the guiding thread of his philosophy in general: 'Everything is good when it springs from the hands of our Creator; everything degenerates when shaped by the hands of man' (P iv. 245, E 37). He conceived *Émile*'s central

11

theme as a plan of education according to Nature rather than art, in which the impulses of the child are allowed to develop, each in its good time, rather than be forced, shaped prematurely, or subjected to exogenous control, by precept or instruction. Rousseau here maps out a genetic account of the spiritual growth of the individual along lines which reflect his evolutionary perspective, in the second *Discourse*, of our passage from a savage to a civilized state, albeit in *Émile* around images of sentiment and sexuality rather than of reason and authority. But in the blossoming of the child's faculties, the rule that he must initally depend only on things and not upon men offers him the prospect of an education entirely distinct from that which must have led to the corruption of the human race in the past. *Émile* was the first of Rousseau's works to point the way to a form of independence which might still be achieved by individuals even in corrupt society, from whose grip escape might now be contemplated, by the cultivation of self-reliance. To that extent the work displays a cautious, if unfulfilled, optimism about the prospects of humanity's conceivable development which was not apparent in his earlier writings. No doubt this significant change of tone was partly inspired by Rousseau's own success in emancipating himself from the trappings of Parisian society.

According to his *Confessions*, however, the first work to which he turned in his new home was the *Social Contract*, a composition which he had already begun to plan while in Venice, and which he was now resolved to assemble into the finest of all his writings. The principles of the true social contract are perhaps best understood in contradiction with the sinister formula of agreement recounted in the second *Discourse*—such a contract, when properly construed, fulfilling rather than destroying the true liberty of citizens, by rendering them equal under law instead of subservient to their appointed political masters. Liberty and equality together are the two principles that ought to be main objects of every system of legislation, Rousseau proclaims here, and much of the *Social Contract* is devoted to explaining why that should be so. Having already differentiated the moral and political from the natural and physical spheres of our lives, Rousseau contends that distinct forms of liberty or freedom are appropriate to each. Without government, he argues, men can be naturally free in the sense of not being subject to the will of others, but their freedom is attached merely to the satisfaction of their organic impulses. Only in political society, whose establishment requires that our natural liberty be abandoned, can we realize either civil or moral liberty, of which the first makes us dependent upon the whole community and the second obedient to laws that express our own collective will. In the *Social Contract* he claims that the state could serve as the instrument of freedom only when all its subjects were at the same time sovereign, for then alone can the people be truly said to rule themselves. Only when each of the state's citizens takes direct part in legislation can they jointly check the abuse of power which some of them might seek to wield, he observes, and while a number of his contemporaries, such as Montesquieu and Voltaire, had praised the liberal principles enshrined in the British Constitution, he instead judged the English system of parliamentary rule incompatible with the electorate's freedom, in delegating the people's sovereignty to their representatives.

After the publication of his *Social Contract*, Rousseau drafted a *Constitution for Corsica* in 1765 and an essay on *The Government of Poland* around 1771, in both instances on the invitation of leading citizens of those fledgling regimes, who invited him to serve as their legislator. If Corsica had escaped invasion, and Poland its partitions, it might have been possible, in the late eighteenth century, to witness how the principles of the *Social Contract* could be applied to the constitutions of actual states. He had always intended that this should be the case, he claimed, in seeking the conjunction of political theory and practice, as much as his French Revolutionary admirers later, albeit in a different way. Contrasting his philosophy with that of Plato and also More, he maintained that he had not put forward an unworldly utopian ideal. On the contrary, his *Social Contract* had been intended to elucidate the theoretical foundations of an object close to home, in particular the constitution of Geneva, and it was just because that constitution had been forsaken, he believed, that he had incurred the wrath of the current authorities of his native state (P iii. 810). This was one of the main arguments of his third major work devoted largely to politics, his *Letters from the Mountain* of 1764.

The feature of his *Social Contract* which, in his lifetime, aroused the deepest public fury, however, was its penultimate chapter on the civil religion. Rousseau there stresses the significance of a religious as well as political foundation for our civic responsibilities, according to which citizens perform and love their duty as a matter of patriotic faith, joining them together in common devotion to an almighty, benign, and tolerant Divinity. This aspect of his thought, partly inspired by his beloved Machiavelli, brought Rousseau into conflict both with the religious and political establishment of his day and with many of its leading critics. To *philosophes* intent upon reforming the *Ancien Régime*, his religious zealotry seemed yet again a betrayal of the Enlightenment and a dark reinvocation of blind faith in a dawning age of reason. On the other hand, his express condemnation of Christianity, which he describes as best suited to tyrannical government, outraged the Church and political authorities alike. His 'Profession of Faith of the Savoyard Vicar' in *Émile*, moreover, which appeared at almost the same time as the *Social Contract*, set forth the fullest and most eloquent statement of his philosophy of natural as opposed to revealed religion, and that dismayed those authorities even more.

From their censure Rousseau was never really to recover. Both *Émile* and the *Social Contract* were banned or confiscated in Paris and burnt in Geneva. Forced to flee from the one city and subject to arrest in the other, he found himself in 1762 a fugitive from justice, surprised both at the vehemence of the official reaction to claims which he thought would be attributed to truly Christian scruples, in contrast with the atheism of so many *philosophes*, and at the initial failure of his compatriots to come to his aid. In May 1763, in despair, having found temporary refuge in Môtiers, near Neuchâtel, under the nominal jurisdiction of Frederick the Great of Prussia, he repudiated his Genevan citizenship. Thereafter he remained homeless, often obliged to travel incognito, at the mercy of protectors whose real aim, he sometimes suspected, was to ensnare and malign him. One such protector was to be David Hume, who in January 1766 personally accompanied Rousseau to England, where he stayed almost eighteen months, principally at Wootton, in Staffordshire—in that time, overwhelmed by suspicions of an international conspiracy to discredit his character, managing to bring great misery upon himself, and much discomfort to Hume. Real persecution compounded the paranoia with which he was undoubtedly afflicted at least from the mid-1760s, and for the rest of his life he was convinced that his former companions in the vanguard of the Enlightenment—Diderot, d'Alembert, d'Holbach, and Grimm—assisted by Voltaire and his patrician friends, who had always loathed him, were in league with his political enemies in a monumental network of conspiracy against him. Having returned to France on an undertaking to desist from publishing his writings, he found respite only in solitude, the study of botany, and a romantically lyrical communion with Nature, as recounted in his last major work, for some readers his greatest masterpiece, the *Reveries*, which would appear posthumously with the first part of his *Confessions*. In 1778, soon after being drawn yet again to a refuge just north of Paris, at Ermenonville, provided by the Marquis de Girardin, he died of apoplexy, 'without uttering a single word', his widow reports (L 8344), contradicting groundless suggestions that he had committed suicide.

Yet while Rousseau had become estranged from mainstream Enlightenment thinkers, he had a great many passionate followers as well, throughout France and among radical circles in Geneva and above all, perhaps, in enlightened Europe's peripheries—Italy, Scotland, and Germany, where Kant and Goethe were to prove the most prominent of his admirers of the next generation or two. In the course of the French Revolution, especially, when the manuscript of his *Confessions* was presented to the Convention and his body was ceremoniously transported to Paris, his influence upon eighteenth-century life and thought was at its zenith. No other figure of his age had more clearly expressed the Revolutionaries' commitment to the principles of liberty, equality, and fraternity, nor a deeper devotion to the ideal of popular sovereignty, whose adoption in France signalled an end to the *Ancien Régime*. In the political career of the Incorruptible Robespierre in particular—his opposition to patronage and to priestly theology, his patriotic zeal and promotion of the Cult of the Supreme Being—can be found, as well as much else besides, the most zealous practical exposition of Rousseau's doctrines. Rousseau himself never advocated revolution, judged political uprisings worse than the disease they were intended to cure, and held little hope for the political salvation of mankind. But he foresaw Europe's impending crisis and the advent of a revolutionary age, hoping it might be averted. When the French Revolution was launched a decade after his death, many of its leaders nevertheless drew up their programmes and constitutions in the fiery light of his philosophy.

2 Culture, Music, and the Corruption of Morals

Rousseau remarks in his *Confessions* that he had been thunderstruck on reading the notice of the Academy of Dijon in the *Mercure de France* of October 1749, heralding a competition for the best essay on the question 'Has the rebirth of the arts and sciences contributed to the purification of morals?'. 'The moment I read this announcement I saw another universe and became a different man', he writes (P i. 351, C 327). He had stopped by a tree to catch his breath, moved almost to delirium by a fiery vision of the natural goodness of humanity and the evil contradictions of our social order, which had kindled in his mind most of the leading ideas of what would become his principal works, even though he was never to recapture more than its faint shadow. Yet while the *Discourse on the Arts and Sciences* forms the most immediate expression of that vision, Rousseau eventually came to regard it as among the worst of his major writings. The text which launched his literary career had neither order, nor logic, nor structure, he lamented, and, though it was full of warmth and vigour, it was, on his own testimony, the feeblest and least elegant of his celebrated works (P i. 352, C 328–9). It is also, as was soon to be noted by his detractors, the least original.

Its central theme is that civilization has been the bane of humanity, and that the perfection of our arts and sciences has been accompanied by the corruption of our morals. Before we acquired the skills and attributes of cultured men, and before our patterns of life came to be moulded by false values and factitious needs, our manners were 'rustic but natural'. With the birth and dissemination of knowledge, however, our original purity became progressively debased by sophistical taste and custom, by the 'perfidious veil of politeness', and by 'all those vicious ornaments' of fashion, until our pristine virtue had been wrenched away with the force of an ebbing tide (P iii. 8, 10, 21; G 6, 7, 18). We cannot but regret our loss of the simplicity of that earliest epoch when our forebears had lived together in huts and sought little more than the approval of their gods, Rousseau maintains. In the beginning the world's only adornments would have been sculpted by Nature herself, and thereafter it has been those civilizations which remain closest to Her, least burdened by the trappings of culture and learning, which have proved the most vigorous and robust. Our arts and sciences, he observes, do not inspire individuals with courage or the spirit of patriotism; on the contrary they sap men of both their devotion to the state and their strength to preserve it from invasion. Since the marvellous inventions of the Chinese failed to ward off their subjection to the coarse and ignorant Tartars, the erudition of their sages was manifestly useless. On the other hand, the Persians, who mastered virtue rather than science, were easily able to conquer Asia, while the greatness of the German and Scythian nations was firmly grounded on the simplicity, innocence, and patriotic spirit of their inhabitants (P iii. 11, 22; G 9, 18).

Above all, the history of Sparta, when contrasted with that of Athens, demonstrates how much more durable and resistant to the vices of tyranny are those communities which have been spared the vain monuments of culture. Socrates, the wisest person in Athens, cautioned his fellow citizens of the dangerous consequences of their arrogance, and later, at Rome, Cato followed his example and inveighed against the venomously seductive delights of art and ostentation that undermined the vitality of his compatriots. Yet each man's warnings went unheeded, and an entirely specious form of learning came to prevail in both Athens and Rome, to the detriment of military discipline, agricultural production, and political vigilance. The Roman Republic, in particular, once the temple of virtue, soon became the decadent theatre of crime, slowly succumbing under the yoke with which it had earlier harnessed its barbarian captives. Much the same pattern of decline had also marked the collapse of the ancient empires of Egypt, Greece, and Constantinople, Rousseau adds, proclaiming it a general rule that all great civilizations decay under the weight of their scientific and artistic progress (P iii. 10–14, G 8–12).

The first *Discourse* offers little explanation of these developments, however, barely sketching the way the arts and sciences could have been so comprehensively responsible for the moral decadence of man. On the one hand, all our sciences, Rousseau suggests, have been formed out of idleness, each discipline stemming from the vices to which indolence gives rise—astronomy from superstition, for instance, geometry from avarice, and physics from excessive curiosity. On the other hand, our arts are everywhere nourished by luxury, which is itself born out of sloth and the vanity of men. Luxury is presented as a crucial feature, since Rousseau maintains that it can seldom thrive in the absence of the arts and sciences, while they never exist without it. According to his argument, it seems that the dissolution of morals must have been a necessary consequence of luxury, which, in turn, stemmed from idleness, with the human corruption and enslavement which have been such characteristic features of the history of all civilizations presented as appropriate punishment for our swollen endeavour to advance beyond that state of happy ignorance in which it would have been a blessing to remain for ever (P iii. 15, 17–19, 21; G 13–16, 18).

In all these respects, the *Discourse on the Arts and Sciences* comprises the first major statement of the philosophy of history—to the effect that our apparent cultural and social progress has led only to our real moral degradation—which Rousseau was to develop as one of the most central themes of his works. But in the first *Discourse* that philosophy of history still appears rudimentary and obscure, comprised, as it is there, of at least three distinct theses about the course and circumstances of our corruption: first, the suggestion that mankind has declined progressively from the innocence of its earliest primitive state; second, the claim that nations which are artistically and scientifically underdeveloped are morally superior to their sophisticated counterparts; and third, the contention that great civilizations have become decadent under the weight of their own cultural progress. To his readers, these propositions seemed not to accord easily with one another, especially since the tribute Rousseau pays to the mode of life of primitive man, on the one hand, and to robust civilization which succeeds savage society, on the other, is compounded by his further proposition—so fashionable in the Enlightenment—that human history had been interrupted by a reversion, under several centuries of medieval barbarism and superstition, to a state deemed worse than that of our original ignorance. At the end of his text

Rousseau even launches upon an entirely new thesis to the effect that it is not really the arts and sciences as such but rather their abuse by persons of ordinary talent which has been the true source of our misfortunes, and he actually concludes his work with the observation that great scientists and artists should be entrusted with the task of building monuments to honour the glory of the human spirit. The rest of us lesser mortals, he exclaims, should aspire to no more than the obscurity and mediocrity to which we have been destined. It is difficult to grasp why Rousseau should have thought such sentiments appropriate to a critique of the arts and sciences and a defence of the virtues of ignorance, innocence, and common humanity (P iii. 6, 22, 29–30; G 4, 18, 25–6).

Nor was he clear as to the precise nature of the contribution which he believed the growth of culture had made to our decline. His thesis appeared to be quite simply that the progress of the arts and sciences has been responsible for the debasement of morals, but he also supposed that the arts and sciences were nourished by the indolence, vanity, and luxury to which men aspire and which some enjoy. Had the advancement of culture been the cause of our corruption, then, or its effect? Rousseau, whose main concern in the work is to portray the evils which invariably derive from the pursuit of culture and knowledge, but who equally proclaims that our arts and sciences owe their origin to our vices (P iii. 17, 19; G 14, 16), seems to have been unable to make up his mind.

One of the reasons for his irresolution may be the fact that so many features of his argument were borrowed from earlier thinkers, such as Montesquieu, Fénelon, Montaigne, Seneca, Plato, and, above all, Plutarch, whose writings he had read at length, and whose commentaries on the superiority of nature over artifice, or the oppressiveness of inequality, or the decadence of civilization, were endorsed or recapitulated in his text. In his *Essay on the Reigns of Claudius and Nero* Diderot later remarked that 'a hundred apologies for ignorance in the face of the arts' and sciences' advance had been made before Rousseau', and he was certainly correct. But the first *Discourse* lacks originality not only because it bears the general influence of other works in a similar vein to which Rousseau turned for guidance, or because his scholarship is plainly second-hand—his account of the Scythians, for instance, drawn essentially from Horace, his description of the Germans from Tacitus, his sketch of the Persians from Montaigne, and his contrast between Sparta and Athens from several writers, but most especially Bossuet and the historian Charles Rollin. Its derivative character is due above all to the fact that the very words Rousseau employs to express his principal ideas were often borrowed from his authorities. Apart from the numerous references whose sources are manifestly clear, there is at least one passage in the *Discourse on the Arts and Sciences* drawn, without acknowledgement, from Montesquieu's *Spirit of the Laws* and one unattributed transcription from Bossuet's *Discourse on Universal History*; there are several snatches from Plutarch's *Lives* and upwards of fifteen extracts from the *Essays* of Montaigne, only a few of which allude to their source; the very last line of Rousseau's text is adapted from both Plutarch and Montaigne together. Dom Joseph Cajot's *Plagiarisms of Rousseau*, published in 1766, may have been excessively severe—and in most instances incorrect—in its imputations, but it remains the case that the *Discourse on the Arts and Sciences* is the only one of Rousseau's writings which invites such suspicions. Despite the polemical tone and character of the argument, it is directed against no other work in particular, and Rousseau appears to have turned to his sources more in order to recapitulate them than to lend weight to his own ideas. The difference between his first and second *Discourse* with regard to this point could hardly be more stark, since in the *Discourse on Inequality* he was to embark on a refutation of most of the figures mentioned in his text, whereas in the *Discourse on the Arts and Sciences* he managed little more than to reflect, albeit perhaps in a more powerful idiom of his own, the disparate views already advanced by its precursors. His first major work enunciates a philosophy of history to which he was to adhere for the rest of his life and which his contemporaries, at least, came to recognize as his most central doctrine. It was the first of his writings emblazoned with his signature 'Citizen of Geneva', thereby proclaiming his proud identity and authorship. Yet in launching his literary career, it was to prove his least characteristic, least personal, achievement.

Rousseau's development as a writer, nevertheless, owed much to the dispute which exploded around his *Discourse on the Arts and Sciences* immediately following its publication and which raged for at least three years thereafter. In the course of that controversy, by way of attempting to vindicate his work against his critics, he came to assemble, elaborate, and refine his original claims in a manner that was often different from their first formulation. He made no effort to reply to all his detractors, but he tried to rebut at least six works in particular that came to his notice. Several of his critics charged that he had failed to specify the precise point of our moral decline, so that he had given the impression of preferring Europe's centuries of barbarism to the renaissance of the sciences which followed, and a few decried his general lack of scholarship, in his misunderstanding of the brutal nature of the ancient Scythians, or his neglect of the fact that some of the figures he had praised, such as Seneca, believed that virtue was enhanced and not debased by literature. To these allegations Rousseau retorted, particularly in a 'Letter to the abbé Raynal', that his aim had been to put forward a general thesis about the connection between artistic and scientific advance, on the one hand, and moral decadence, on the other, rather than to trace the course of any particular set of events, so that such critics had misunderstood the purpose of his work (P iii. 31–2, G 28–9).

He was to pursue this theme of generality much further in his *Discourse on Inequality*, where he shifts his attention from the untainted civilizations of the ancient world to the nature of primeval man and to a condition of humanity so remote that *no* historical research could possibly uncover its true features. After the publication of his first *Discourse*, Rousseau was to become progressively more concerned with the ultimate sources of our decadence and less with its particular manifestations in different cultures. Paradoxically, however, while he gradually set his sights upon our most distant past, his evidence came to be drawn from an increasingly contemporary world, in effect populated by savages who had thus far escaped the miseries of human history rather than by the heroes and sages of antiquity. By the mid-1750s, that is, his fidelity to the venerable *Lives* of Plutarch came at least to be counterbalanced by a new enthusiasm for the *General History of Voyages*, edited by the author of *Manon Lescaut*, the abbé Prévost. As the divisions between man's nature and culture which Rousseau perceived grew sharper and bolder, so too did the arguments he put forward to portray these differences, and in the course of the development of his early social theory the deficiencies of his historical scholarship were soon to be overcome by the breadth and sweep of his speculative insights into the general plight of our species as a whole.

Several of the critics of his first *Discourse* also accused him of resuscitating the nostalgic chimera of an ancient golden age, which had existed in myth and poetry but never in fact. To this objection Rousseau replied, especially in his answer to Borde's *Discourse on the Advantages of the Arts and Sciences* of 1751, that the idea of an ancient golden age was not a historical illusion but a philosophical abstraction, no more chimerical in substance, and no less necessary for our self-understanding and well-being, than the concept of virtue itself (P iii. 80, G 73). He had not juxtaposed past and present epochs of our history in order to encourage the rescue of fictitious virtues or the lost innocence of antiquity. In two of his works stemming from the first *Discourse*, the 'Observations' addressed to King Stanislaw of Poland and the preface to his play *Narcissus*, he observes that a people, once it was corrupted, could never return to a virtuous state, and this was a thesis to which he was to subscribe throughout his life. Above all, he took great offence at the suggestion, first made by the mathematician and historian Joseph Gautier, that he had become an apologist of ignorance who appeared to believe that our culture should be crushed and our libraries burnt. Of course we must not plunge Europe back into a state of barbarism, he responds, nor was he advocating the obliteration of our libraries, academies, or universities, least of all the destruction of society itself (P ii. 971–2; P iii. 55–6, 95; G 50–1, 88, 108). Reversion to a natural state is no more possible for civilized man than would be the recovery of innocence or ignorance of vice. Following such objections to his *Discourse on the Arts and Sciences*, Rousseau was always to stress that the morally upright citizen must attempt to make his way in *this* world rather than in some ancient paradise of remote imagination. The alternative course of solitude and communion with Nature which he would personally espouse towards the end of his life was not one he was to recommend as a strategy for disenchanted subjects of modern states, and he remained adamant that his ideas were neither utopian nor violent in their implications.

He was impressed by the force of some of the objections raised by his critics, and occasionally modified or abandoned certain features of his theory in the light of them. Thus when King Stanislaw of Poland challenged his account of the connection between virtue and ignorance, on the grounds that uncultured men whom Rousseau had applauded were sometimes brutal rather than benign, he accepted the point and proposed a distinction between two forms of ignorance, of which one was odious and terrible, and the other modest and pure (P iii. 53–4, G 48–9). Yet without further elaboration this reply was hardly convincing, and in his later writings he was to prove more hesitant in ascribing the moral innocence of primitive men to their mere lack of learning. The philosopher Charles Borde, whom Rousseau had befriended in the early 1740s, claimed that the author of the *Discourse on the Arts and Sciences* had also been unwise to praise the military prowess of uncivilized peoples, whose barbarous conquests stemmed from injustice rather than innocence. Rousseau was quick to concur, allowing that it is not our natural destiny to destroy one another. Although he at first suggests that devotion to war for the sake of conquest is unlike willingness to fight for the defence of liberty (P iii. 82, G 75), he was never again to portray the ideal of military valour in quite the shining colours he had employed in the first *Discourse*. He did not abandon his belief, inspired by Machiavelli, that the liberties of the Roman Republic had been sustained by its citizens' militia, but in the *Discourse on Inequality* and afterwards he was to portray all wars as criminal, murderous, execrable, and—for the combatants themselves—pointless.

While Rousseau thus made a few concessions to his critics, he turned other charges to more productive use in the development of his theory. This is particularly true of his replies to the claims of Stanislaw and Borde that the moral degradation of man was attributable to an excess of wealth rather than learning, and of his response to Borde's contention that the decline of nations could ultimately be due only to political causes. In his 'Observations' he acknowledges that such factors as the customs of different peoples and their climate, laws, economies, and governments (to which d'Alembert had drawn attention in objecting to Rousseau's thesis in his 'Preliminary Discourse' to the *Encyclopédie* of 1751) must all have figured in the formation of peoples' moral traits (P iii. 42–3, G 38), and thereafter he begins to address the impact of such factors more directly. In his 'Last Reply' to Borde, of 1752, for instance, he notes that luxury, which he had earlier condemned as the principal cause of our decadence, was itself due largely to the decline of agriculture in the modern world (P iii. 79, G 72). In the same text, and subsequently in his preface to *Narcissus*, he draws attention for the first time in his writings to the nefarious influence of private property. In the 'Last Reply' he deals mainly with the concept of ownership, and with the brutal division of the earth between masters and slaves which the practical application of that concept entails, largely in order to challenge Borde's thesis that men in their most primitive state must already have been fierce and aggressive. 'Before those dreadful words *thine* and *mine* were invented', he exclaims, 'before there were men so abominable as to crave for superfluities while others starve of hunger', I should like to know just what our ancestors' vices could have been (P iii. 80, G 73). In the preface to *Narcissus* he concentrates instead upon the fact that the moral attributes of the savage were markedly superior to those of the European, because savages were unscathed by the habitual vices of greed, envy, and deception which in the civilized world have caused men to scorn and to make enemies of one another. 'The word *property*', he reflects there, 'has almost no meaning among savages'. 'They have no conflicting interests around it; nothing drives them to deceive each other', as covetous civilized men always do (P ii. 969–70 n., G 106 n.). In these two passages directed against the critics of his *Discourse on the Arts and Sciences*, we thus find Rousseau's earliest major statements of the thesis which he was later to expound in the form of a challenge—on that occasion to Locke's theory of property—in the *Discourse on Inequality*.

Rousseau was now beginning to look more closely at the role of political factors as well. The evils of contemporary society had been described before by many figures, he reflects in the preface to *Narcissus*, but while others had perceived the problem, he had actually uncovered its causes, and the essential truth he had learnt by 1753 was that all our vices stem ultimately not from our nature but from the ways in which we have been badly governed (P ii. 969, G 106). He was to make the same point again two years later in his *Discourse on Political Economy*, where he remarks that 'Peoples are in the long run what their governments make of them' (P iii. 251, H 10). He was to stress it once more in the following decade in his *Letter to Christophe de Beaumont*, where he proclaims that the counterfeit behaviour of civilized men is caused by our 'social order', which brings continual tyranny to bear upon our nature (P iv. 966). And around 1770 he was to reflect in his *Confessions* that the truth of this principle had already been apparent to him thirty years earlier, during his sojourn in Venice, when he had witnessed the dire consequences for its people which followed from the defects of that nation's government. The preface to *Narcissus* thus embraces the first statement of an idea whose elaboration in several contexts and in different forms was to occupy a major part of Rousseau's life and works.

With regard to the contribution made by wealth and riches to our moral decline, Rousseau soon showed himself to be only partly in accord with the ideas of Stanislaw and Borde. In several fragmentary writings of the early 1750s, especially a short piece on 'Luxury, Commerce, and the Arts', he acknowledges that the cupidity of man is a manifestation of his desire to set himself above his neighbours, so that the introduction of gold in human affairs had been unavoidably accompanied by the inequality of its distribution, from which there then issued the vice of poverty and the humiliation of the poor by the rich (P iii. 522). But even in recognizing the part played by the accumulation of riches in mankind's moral corruption, he insists that it was not the principal cause of our decline. On the contrary, as he declares in his 'Observations', wealth and poverty are relative terms which reflect rather than determine the extent of inequality in society. Rearranging the genealogy of vices which he had portrayed in the first *Discourse*, he now proposes that pride of place in the dismal order of our corruption should be granted to inequality, which was then followed by wealth, which in turn made possible the growth of luxury and indolence, which then gave rise to the arts, on the one hand, and to the sciences, on the other (P iii. 49–50, G 44–5). Here was a new version of his argument, placing the arts and sciences last, and not first, as his critics supposed.

At least part of the reason for this modification of his views may be gleaned from his 'Observations' and the preface to *Narcissus*, where he suggests that while the progress of culture has been responsible for a whole train of vices, it is fundamentally our *desire* to shine through learning rather than the achievement of learned men which undermines our morals in civilized society. For our pursuit of culture above all else expresses our resolve to distinguish ourselves from our neighbours and compatriots, he claims, in both places elaborating a brief remark about 'the rage for distinction' which figures in the first *Discourse* itself, recollecting perhaps the main thrust of Fénelon's most central contribution to the quarrel of the ancients and moderns which had fermented in France for more than thirty years around the turn of the eighteenth century. It is not so much our devotion to excellence as our wish to command the respect of others that has prompted us to manufacture the artefacts and instruments of advanced societies, so that civilization seems only a fulfilment of our attempts to establish an unequal distribution of public esteem (P ii. 965; P iii. 19, 48; G 16, 43, 102). Moral virtue cannot truly exist, Rousseau contends, unless individual shares of talent are roughly equal. The only safeguard which we had ever had against corruption, he remarks in his 'Observations', was that original equality, now irredeemably lost, which had once conserved our innocence and been the source of virtue (P iii. 56, G 51). Thus does he conclude that our craving for distinction in the arts and sciences is a manifestation of much the same factitious feeling as the desire to dominate in politics—a sentiment upon which he would soon focus his attention in the *Discourse on Inequality*.

In all these respects, therefore, Rousseau's replies to the critics of his *Discourse on the Arts and Sciences* led him towards the more political, social, and economic lines of argument that he was to pursue in the second *Discourse* and beyond. Yet he never abandoned his earlier views about the importance of the arts and sciences as causal agents of human corruption. On the contrary, throughout the dispute surrounding his *Discourse on the Arts and Sciences*, he consistently reaffirms the claims which he had made in his prize essay about the interconnections between vanity, sloth, luxury, and culture, even while extending his argument to accommodate other factors. One of his critics, Claude-Nicolas Le Cat, a professor of anatomy and surgery and Permanent Secretary of the Academy of Rouen, managed to provide Rousseau with a whole new front for the development of his ideas, in challenging him to be more precise as to which areas of culture were subject to his imputations. Surely Rousseau did not propose to include music among those arts and sciences which had brought about our degradation, Le Cat exclaimed, confident that the *Encyclopédie's* principal contributor on musical subjects must know better than anyone else how useful and advantageous this art has been, and how, at the very least, it must form an exception to his general thesis.

Le Cat's supposition could scarcely have been further from the truth. In 1753, at the height of the *Querelle des Bouffons*, the controversy surrounding Pergolesi's *Serva padrona* and Italian *opera buffa* which divided the patrons of the Paris Opéra and the French Court into musical factions, Rousseau produced his *Letter on French Music*, which provoked an even greater storm of protest than the *Discourse on the Arts and Sciences* three years earlier. Some languages, Rousseau contends there, are more appropriate to music than others, on account of their more mellifluous vowels, their more gentle inflections, and their more precisely measured figures of speech. Such languages, above all Italian in particular, he claims, lend themselves to clear melodic intonations and to expression in song. Other languages, like French, are marked by a lack of sonorous vowels and by consonants so coarse that agreeable tunes cannot be sung in them, leaving composers from nations with such a speech impediment obliged to embellish their music with the strident noise of harmonic accompaniment. Articulation of the French language in unadorned song is thus impossible, and if the people of France should ever seek a form of music of their own, he concludes in the last line of his text, so much the worse for them. Following this provocative work and these defamatory remarks, Rousseau was to be hanged in effigy for his affront to public taste. If his *Letter on French Music* did not quite excite an insurrection, it made him appear, for the first time in his life, an enemy of the French state. As Voltaire was later to recognize, Rousseau is nowhere so politically inflammatory as when commenting on music.

If Le Cat had been able to read the section devoted to that subject which Rousseau originally drafted as a part of the *Discourse on Inequality*, and which eventually appeared posthumously in 1781 as two chapters of the *Essay on the Origin of Languages*, he would have understood why music could form no exception to Rousseau's general thesis of the *Discourse on the Arts and*

Sciences. On the contrary, the corruption of human morality was *most* clearly manifested, according to Rousseau, in the history of the development of music. Our first languages, he contends in the *Essay*, probably arose in the southern regions of the world, where the climate was mild and the land fertile. They must have had a rhythmic and melodic character and would have been poetic rather than prose, sung rather than spoken, so that in their first articulations of impulsive passions our forebears must, in short, have been enchanting (G 271–2, 276, 282). But languages which would subsequently have arisen in the inclement conditions of the north would have first expressed men's needs rather than their passions and would have been less sonorous and more shrill (G 245, 273–5). With the eventual conquest of the Mediterranean world under a wave of barbarian invasions, the guttural and staccato speech of northern men must have taken precedence over the mellifluous intonations which had served for the expression of human sentiments before, and all the sweetness, measure, and grace of our original languages would have been lost (G 291–2). The melodic forms of diction would have been suppressed, Rousseau claims, and our utterances would have been progressively deprived of their initial charm. Under the bondage of barbarian rule and agricultural labour, humdrum prose would in effect have taken precedence over poetic song, and with the emergence of prose, languages, particularly the earliest forms of French, English, and German, accordingly would have become prosaic (G 258, 275). Music, on the other hand, would have been rendered senseless by the loss of its semantic component appropriated by the languages of prose, and it would have come to be developed further only by the Gothic innovation of harmony, implanting chordal patterns upon the utterances of men that yielded artificial pleasures in place of the natural delights of vernacular song. Under these pressures music would have become more instrumental than vocal, and the calculation of intervals would have been substituted for the finesse of melodic inflections (G 290). Prose, on the other hand, would have come to be refined in writing rather than speech, communicated no longer with expressive force but only the exactitude of grammatical rules and a precise dictionary of terms, which it would have been necessary to consult in order to ascertain one's feelings (G 251, 281).

As if to meet Le Cat's challenge to his philosophy of history, Rousseau entitled the final chapter of his essay 'The Relation of Languages to Government' and proclaims there that languages which have come to be separated from music are inimical to freedom. A prosaic rhetoric inspires servile manners, and speech made hollow by its lack of tone and rhythm, he asserts, also makes for hollow men. The languages of modern Europe have become suitable only for discourse at close quarters, as the ineffectual chatter of persons who just murmur feebly to one another with voices which lack inflection, and therefore spirit and passion as well. As our speech has succumbed to the loss of its musical traits it has been deprived of its original vigour and clarity and become little more than the faint mutterings of individuals who have no strength of character or purpose. And if this is the private aspect of our contemporary languages, their public manifestation, according to Rousseau, is more oppressive still. For men who govern others but have nothing to say themselves can do little else when the people are assembled apart from shout and preach to them, in intemperate and unintelligible pronouncements. The proclamations of our rulers and the supplications of our priests continually abuse our sensibilities and make us numb, and tortuous harangues and sermons, delivered by both secular and religious charlatans, have become the sole form of popular oratory in the modern world (G 294–5).

Both the private and public faces of language, Rousseau concludes, thus provide an accurate portrait of the utterly degraded state into which our societies have fallen. Conversation has become covert, political discourse has become barren, and we have all succeeded in bringing our original manner of speaking up to date only by becoming the speechless auditors of those who rule by diatribes and recitations from the pulpit. In fact since even these perverted forms of rhetoric are no longer necessary to keep us in our allotted places, the rulers of modern states have correctly come to understand that they can maintain their authority without convening any popular meetings or assemblies at all. They have only to direct the attention of their subjects to the many things which they might exchange with each other and away from the few thoughts that they might still wish to communicate, so that in their latest form the vocal intonations which had once expressed our pleasures have been reconstituted as the terms that denote our trades. Whereas the words *aimez-moi* must in the past have been superseded by *aidez-moi*, now all that we say to each other is *donnez de l'argent* (G 273–4, 294). In book iii, chapter 15 of the *Social Contract* Rousseau would later pursue much the same argument, shorn of its musical but not its political dimension.

Of course the *Essay on the Origin of Languages* must have been inspired by much more besides Le Cat's objection to the *Discourse on the Arts and Sciences*. On Rousseau's own testimony it originally formed a section of the *Discourse on Inequality*, which he withdrew because it was too long and out of place and which in 1755 he then appended to a study of the *Principle of Melody* that he had drafted in reply to Rameau, only to withdraw it once again. Its contrast between melody and harmony forms a central strain of the critique of Rameau's philosophy of music which he developed in this period of his life, and which, in its turn, had been prompted by a number of works advancing the case for the supremacy of harmony over melody that Rameau had produced partly in criticism of Rousseau's articles on music for the *Encyclopédie*. But it forms an intrinsic part of his philosophy of history as well, and comprises a more richly drawn illustration of his claim that the progress of civilization has led to the corruption of morals than can be found in his discussion of any of the other arts or sciences. To that extent it takes up Le Cat's challenge to his original thesis most directly. In a note of his 'Last Reply' to Borde, Rousseau claims that he had foreseen and dealt in advance with all his detractors' plausible complaints against his case (P iii. 71–2, G 65), but he thereby does scant justice to their ingenuity or to the subtlety of his own rejoinders, whose fresh themes are largely imperceptible in his original text.

At least one objection to the first *Discourse*, however, was to remain unanswered in Rousseau's early writings. An anonymous critic—possibly the abbé Raynal, who was later to collaborate with Diderot and others in compiling a massive *History of the Two Indies*—complained that Rousseau had failed to offer any practical conclusions following from his thesis and had neglected to propose a remedy for the condition he described. In his 'Last Reply' to Borde, Rousseau acknowledges the force of this criticism and remarks only that he had seen the evil and had tried to locate its sources. The search for a remedy, he claims at this stage of his life, was a task he must leave to others (P iii. 95, G 88). He did not take up the challenge in his *Discourse on Inequality* nor anywhere else in his writings of the early and mid-1750s, but neither did he abandon it completely. In certain works of that period or soon afterwards which were not destined for publication, he could permit his imagination to soar in political reverie which might appear to counsel radical change, as in the second chapter of book i of his *Manuscrit de Genève*, an early version of the *Social Contract* drafted in response to some remarks of Diderot in the *Encyclopédie*, where he calls for the establishment of 'new associations to correct . . . the defect of society in general' (P iii. 288, H 110). Subsequently in his *Letter to d'Alembert*, and in the final version of his *Social Contract*, by way of attempting to breathe new life into ideals of civil association that mankind had lost, he was to propose a set of principles according to which our moral sentiments might be uplifted rather than debased, only to find the authorities of his native Geneva and adopted France so alarmed as to regard even his presence among them a threat to public order.

3 Human Nature and Civil Society

The *Discourse on the Origins of Inequality* is the most important and substantial of Rousseau's early writings, and with the *Social Contract* and *Émile* it has come to exercise the widest influence of all his works. Its impact on its readers was not so immediate or so tempestuous as the public response which had greeted his *Discourse on the Arts and Sciences* or his *Letter on French Music*, since unlike the first *Discourse* it failed to win the prize of the Academy of Dijon for which it had been entered in a fresh competition, and it lacked the topicality of Rousseau's contribution to the *Querelle des Bouffons*, which had stirred strong feelings among partisans of French and Italian music and politics alike. Less embellished with the merely rhetorical flourishes of these earlier works, it pursues a deeper analysis of civilization and its trappings by way of more rigorous argument, for the first time in a political and social idiom which marks the emergence of Rousseau's philosophy of history in its most mature form. While it attracted some praise and even more hostility from reviewers in France, its greatest impact was probably first felt in Scotland, where Adam Smith was to cast his *Theory of Moral Sentiments* in part as a reply to it, and Lord Monboddo was to construct his case for the humanity of great apes in his *Origin and Progress of Language* in the light of propositions on this subject which it embraced. In Germany, both Kant in his *Idea for a Universal History* and Herder in his *Ideas for a Philosophy of the History of Mankind* were also to draw inspiration from its evolutionary doctrines, Kant particularly from its distinction between the refinement of culture and the cultivation of morality, Herder most especially from its account of the social formation of language. In our own day Claude Lévi-Strauss has deemed it the inaugural Enlightenment contribution to the science of anthropology. Although it surveys a more remote antiquity than any of Rousseau's other writings, it has come to be judged the most radical and progressive of his major works, certainly among those published in his lifetime.

Part of the reason for its commanding that reputation is the critical manner of its assessment of earlier political doctrines, including both ancient and modern conceptions of natural law and contemporary theories of the social contract. While Condillac's philosophy of language and Buffon's natural history receive close attention as well and on certain themes are taken to task, it is the political ideas of Hobbes, Pufendorf, and Locke, above all, which are subjected to sharpest scrutiny and condemned at length by Rousseau in this text. He was convinced that these thinkers had provided an account of the sources of human depravity in terms which were quite generally correct, while misconceiving the true significance of their ideas. On the one hand, they had explained how men in the past might have been deluded into accepting those institutions which had made them morally corrupt, but, on the other hand, they believed that it was each man's duty to uphold such institutions, as if they offered solutions to another— for Rousseau entirely fictitious—problem. His rebuttal of Hobbes, Pufendorf, and Locke was pursued along roughly the following lines.

In the first part of the *Discourse* he contends that there must be *two* kinds of inequality among men, one which is natural or physical, and hence beyond our control, the other moral or political, because it depends upon human choice (P iii. 131, G 138). There is, Rousseau observes, no fundamental link between these two types of inequality, for the claims to dominance put forward by the few who govern the many can have no force unless they are acknowledged to be proper, and that acknowledgement was granted by individuals to other persons rather than bestowed as a gift from Nature. The moral and political divisions which obtain throughout the world are thus never to be justified with reference to any of the physical traits which mark individuals apart. If the opposite were true, then the exercise of force might itself create an obligation to obey, and men would somehow command the respect of their neighbours for the same reason that they arouse their fears. In the *Social Contract* Rousseau was to explain at greater length that force is not the foundation of right, and this is his position in the *Discourse on Inequality* as well. Together with other social contract theorists, he believed that the rules which differentiate persons in society could only come to prevail through their consent, so that the inequalities produced by

Nature must have been *transformed* into such inequalities as were enjoined by man (P iii. 160–1, G 166–7).

Rousseau conceived the central theme of his second *Discourse* as an account of how the human race might have undergone a transformation of this sort. Since in their natural state our ancestors would have had only casual and infrequent contact with each other, he claims that the earliest distinctions between individuals would have been of no consequence. The inequalities established by men themselves, however, formed the dominant features of each community (P iii. 162, 193–4; G 168, 199). In their original condition, our forebears could have had 'no moral relations with or determinate obligations to one another' (P iii. 152, G 159), and since natural man had neither any need for the company of other creatures like himself, nor any wish to hurt them, it was only with the birth of social institutions that his weakness became timidity or his strength a menace to his neighbours. The inequalities which have arisen between persons in society, by contrast, where fixed and determinate relations do prevail, bind individuals together permanently through relations of subservience and command.

Because they had been entirely mistaken in their conceptions of the state of nature, Hobbes, Pufendorf, and Locke, by contrast, had wrongly supposed that all individuals must there be equal in their powers, and each of these thinkers had imagined that as a consequence of this equality every person would be apprehensive of his neighbours and unable to live in safety among them. Men of equal abilities, Hobbes had alleged, could pursue the same objectives only at their peril, for without a common power to keep them in awe, they would be in a state of war (*De cive*, ch. 10; *Leviathan*, ch. 13). In order to achieve peace, he had supposed that men must institute an artificial superior or 'mortal god' with absolute authority to protect each person from the next, so that the pernicious effects of equality might be overcome through the subjection of the whole multitude to the Leviathan. Thus while for Rousseau the inequalities of the natural state must have been entirely *without* significance for mankind, according to Hobbes the fact that there must be equality in a masterless world was of great importance and was one of the reasons which made the attainment of peace there naturally impossible.

For Pufendorf, similarly, men must have been precariously equal in their original condition. Agreeing with Hobbes that we were motivated by selfishness rather than any impulse of benevolence or fellowship, he nevertheless contended that in the state of nature we would have been at the mercy of the elements and of fierce animals, drawn together on account of our frailty and timidity, not positively but negatively, in order to survive (*De jure naturae et gentium*, II. iii. 20). This was Pufendorf's doctrine of *socialitas* or natural sociability—a trait which, he claimed, would have led our ancestors to form communities of ever increasing complexity and sophistication, on account of the limitless capacities and insatiable desires unique to our species. The growth of a political commonwealth would accordingly have been more gradual than Hobbes had imagined, but for Pufendorf it was similarly designed to overcome the perilous instability of our natural condition of equality through our acceptance of the rule of an absolute sovereign. Civil society or civilization, thus conceived, provided a remedy for the barbarous misery of our savage state. Kant would later term such a theory of the genesis of society the doctrine of 'unsocial sociability'.

For Locke, too, it had been the fundamental equality of men in their original condition, 'wherein all power and jurisdiction is reciprocal' (*Second Treatise*, ch. 2), which must have made the tenure of property there uncertain and insecure. Only in civil society, he supposed, where it was constantly defended by a superior power entrusted with its care, could private property be safeguarded and our natural right enforced. While Hobbes's central focus had been the political dimension of peace, Pufendorf's the collective need for security, and Locke's the civil protection of property, the three writers appeared to be in agreement that individuals were naturally unable to survive in the absence of government, and thus that an artificial power must always be established to reduce the dangers which accompany the unfettered equality of mankind.

Rousseau's account of inequality's origins in his second *Discourse* was at least partly designed to contradict these claims. In his view, the superior authorities conceived by Hobbes, Pufendorf, and Locke must have reinforced the antagonisms which set persons apart from one another, and did not overcome such differences.

He believed it was impossible to discover from the works of any of these or other political thinkers *why* men in the state of nature should seek protection from their neighbours, but he thought their ideas collectively did none the less explain *how* individuals might have established as legitimate just those determinate and fixed relations which form the distinctions between them in corrupt society. According to Rousseau, confronting Hobbes in particular, it was true that men must have developed all their social obligations so as to protect their lives and their possessions, but since they could not have been at war, nor owned any property, nor had any ambitions to dominate or any reason to fear one another, in their natural state, it was inconceivable that they should originally have felt the need for such security (P iii. 153–4, G 159–60). The state of nature could have contained no endogenous factors to drive its inhabitants out of it, and sentiments of envy or distrust, which made persons apprehensive for their safety or fearful of losing their possessions, were, in his view, simply not appropriate to men who lived contentedly alone.

In the *Discourse on Inequality* he acknowledges that the idea of private property must have constituted the *most* fundamental principle of obligation, although in so far as savages could not originally have formulated principles of any kind, he insists that such an idea must have arisen some time after they had begun to settle in communities. Pufendorf had been mistaken to suppose that men's natural sociability must have impelled them to live together, since society itself is unnatural and depends upon an agreed vocabulary of signs, that is, a language, which makes the shared framework of intelligible discourse possible. But language, in turn, could not have arisen without a pre-existent society which shaped it and gave a commonly accepted meaning to individual utterances. With language requiring society no less than society requiring language, Rousseau concludes—in a passage on the origins of language devoted above all to the linguistic philosophy of Condillac—that he cannot establish which had come first (P iii. 146, 151; G 153, 157–8).

Condillac, in his *Essay on Human Knowledge* of 1746, had, in Rousseau's view, correctly understood that there could not have been discursive languages in mankind's primitive state, however it was conceived, since linguistic skill can only be acquired with great effort in the course of a long apprenticeship. Together with Rousseau, Condillac had recognized that men's first languages must just have been cries of nature (P iii. 148, G 154; *Essay*, I. ii. 4). But unlike Rousseau he had imagined that such impulsive utterances would have been rudimentary signs of thought, representing our forebears' inchoate association of ideas, for even in the most remote antiquity their use of arbitrary linguistic signs must have referred to something else which is not language. In the *Discourse on Inequality* Rousseau takes issue with this thesis, contending that in their original state individuals could not have begun to conceive thoughts without language, any more than they could have formed society without it (P iii. 147, G 154). Savage men would have required expertise in natural history and metaphysics, he contends, in order to grasp the generic meanings of terms required by even the most primitive linguistic signs (P iii. 149, G 156), since language does not just represent thoughts and images, but articulates and forms an essential part of them, having no independent status of its own.

In the absence of both society and language from our most savage state, the establishment of a right of property, such as Locke had described it, would also have been impossible there. No claims of ownership could have been expressed or understood by men and women until the linguistic rules of social life had first been established, for without some form of language individuals could not have had a conception of what was specifically their own, nor could they have undertaken to respect anything that belonged to others. In fact, the institution of private property, Rousseau remarks, must have depended upon a whole variety of conventions and practices which had evolved in the course of human history. It required not only language but also industry, enterprise, progress, and enlightenment, so that it actually formed what he terms the 'last point of the state of nature' and the first point in the emergence of civil society (P iii. 164, G 170).

Yet if the idea of an exclusive right to land could only be acquired after persons had begun to establish fixed relations with one another, it was still vital for Rousseau that we should recognize the institution built upon that idea as central to all subsequent social relations. 'The first man who, having enclosed a piece of ground, thought up the statement *this is mine* and found people simple enough to believe him . . . was the real founder of civil society', Rousseau observes. Such an impostor, a savage forebear of our species inspired by Locke's perniciously cunning eloquence, would have driven mankind into social subjection, concealing the fact, which Locke had himself recognized before embarking on his case for private ownership, that 'the fruits of the earth belong to us all, and the earth itself to nobody' (P iii. 164, G 170). If civil society had been initially formed to justify men's property relations, it must have been just *these* relations, moreover, which had given rise to war. Land would have become scarce through individual appropriation and inheritance, while there must have been an increase in population, leading to usurpations by the rich, robbery by the poor, and the unbridled passions of both (P iii. 175–6, G 181–2). Just as Locke had been mistaken, therefore, to suppose that men could have established territorial rights of exclusive use and occupancy before they had created any other social institutions, so too Hobbes had failed to see that the property relations formed by men in their communities must be the principal cause of war, Rousseau contends (P iii. 136, 170; G 143, 176). Since individuals could have come to harm one another only after and because they had established divisive property relations, in their original propertyless state they plainly would have had no occasion to inflict injury upon one another or to suffer it at each other's hands.

It was thus Rousseau's view that the social contract devised by men in order to make their property secure could not have been formed in the state of nature, but, on the contrary, must have been a hoax perpetrated in society by the rich upon the poor. Its terms might have seemed superficially plausible, because they would have referred to the impartial rule of law and to the security of every man, but its real aim would have been to establish such order as was necessary to preserve the estates of some persons at the expense of others. By their own agreement, the poor (that is, the great majority of persons) would have been required to repudiate their right to share the wealth which men of property enjoyed, with the effect that in exchange for peace and protection of their lives, as Rousseau puts it, 'All ran headlong to their chains, believing they had secured their liberty' (P iii. 176–7, G 182–3). The notion that 'property is theft', advanced by Proudhon and other socialists in the nineteenth century, owes much to this argument.

As portrayed in Rousseau's fashion, the political doctrines of Hobbes, Pufendorf, and Locke only served the purpose of providing legal recognition of men's moral inequality, enshrining in law, and with the force of artificially established authority, just those antagonistic social relations which in fact require civil society's rules of justice for their control. Hobbes's error, he remarks in book i, chapter 2 of the *Manuscrit de Genève*, had not been his presumption of a state of war among men once they had become sociable, but his having supposed that state natural and due to vices which actually spring from rather than give rise to it (P iii. 288, H 109–10). Each of these three thinkers had, in effect, conceived their ideas as solutions to some problems of which those solutions were in fact the cause (P iii. 184, G 190). Hobbes's and Pufendorf's postulates about our fundamental qualities made us appear so miserable that we could not but admire the peace and justice brought to us by governments which transform us from savages into citizens. And yet when we shut the splendid works of such jurisprudential writers and take stock of men outside them, what do we see?, asks Rousseau in a short essay on 'The State of War', which he probably drafted in the late 1750s, perhaps in connection with his commentaries on the abbé de Saint-Pierre's early eighteenth-century projects to promote perpetual peace. We see everyone 'groaning under an iron yoke', he answers, 'the whole of humanity crushed by a handful of oppressors', everywhere suffering and starvation, with the rich contentedly drinking the blood and tears; and throughout the world nothing but 'the strong holding sway over the weak, armed with the redoubtable strength of the law' (P iii. 608–9, H 42–3). It was with sentiments of this kind, expressed in similarly visceral terms, that Rousseau's radical followers and admirers during the French Revolution came to articulate their consummate contempt for the institutions of the *Ancien Régime*.

Hobbes, Pufendorf, and Locke had overlooked the true significance of their ideas, Rousseau believed, largely because they had subscribed to mistaken views of human nature. They had attributed to savage man a set of traits which he could have acquired only in society, and since they had failed to distinguish our social qualities from our natural endowments, their portraits of our original conduct and behaviour had been too thickly drawn, encrusted with the accretions of our development. Having set themselves the task of explaining the state of nature, Rousseau contends in an important and lengthy footnote of his second *Discourse*, they did not hesitate to transpose their ideas across centuries of time, as if men in isolation already lived amongst their neighbours (P iii. 218, G 224–5). Worse still, they had proposed that some of our most fatal vices should be authorized by law.

What must our forebears have been like, then, stripped of the incubus of our social history, as was the statue of Glaucus, described by Plato in the tenth book of the *Republic*, before it had been disfigured by the ravages of time (P iii. 122, G 129)? In the *Discourse on Inequality*, Rousseau suggests that our savage ancestors must have shared two traits in common with all other animals in the state of nature—first, *amour de soi* or a constant impulse to preserve one's life, and, second, *pitié* or compassion for the suffering of other members of the same species. 'Contemplating the first and most simple operations of the human soul', he writes in the work's preface, 'I think I can perceive in it two principles, prior to reason', of which one concerns our own welfare and preservation, and the other excites a natural repugnance at seeing any other beings suffer pain or death. It is from the agreement of these two principles, without its being necessary to introduce Pufendorf's idea of sociability, that all the rules of natural right appear to be derived, he claims (P iii. 125–6, G 132–3). These attributes must have been prior to reason and sociability, for those latter qualities would have taken a long time to mature, and there could have been no manifest sign of them in our original state. To the extent that natural law philosophers before him had contended that men are fundamentally drawn together by a social disposition whose fulfilment was made possible by their faculty of reason, Rousseau, in the second *Discourse*, thus rejects a natural law foundation of society. He did not accept that humans differ from animals by virtue of their possessing any superior innate quality or principle, so that in response to the prize question posed by the Academy of Dijon—'What is the origin of inequality among men, and is it authorized by natural law?'—he once again replies in the negative, much as he had done in the *Discourse on the Arts and Sciences*. 'It is manifestly against the Law of Nature' that the few should be glutted with superfluities while the multitude lack the barest necessities, he exclaims in concluding the second *Discourse* (P iii. 194, G 199). Inequality is not authorized by natural law, he thought, because natural law does not dictate the rules of human conduct in men's primeval state. The rest of his second *Discourse* forms an attempt to trace the genesis and history of moral inequality in other terms.

Rousseau was convinced that Hobbes in particular had ignored men's *pitié* or natural compassion because he had a misconceived impression of their *amour de soi* or self-love. He had imagined that in order to preserve their lives, individuals were impelled to resist the attempts of others to destroy them, so that it was impossible, in the state of nature, for any man to be both compassionate and secure. But for Rousseau, by contrast, caring properly for oneself does not exclude concern for the welfare of others; on the contrary he believed that a pitiless desire for security at the expense of any person gives rise to just that vanity and contempt which transform mere strangers into enemies. Mandeville, whose theory of human nature in his *Fable of the Bees* of 1714 was similar to that of Hobbes, had perceived that this is so, Rousseau observes, but Hobbes had not (P iii. 154, G 160–1). His conception of self-love was not really that of *amour de soi* but of *amour-propre*, or vanity, a purely relative and factitious feeling which in society prompts individuals to make *more* of themselves than of others and is the source, Rousseau suggests in another important footnote (P iii. 219, G 226), of the 'sense of honour' so crucially, and wrongly, ascribed by Hobbes to human nature in general. While in their undomesticated or uncivilized state both animals and men look out for themselves *and* look kindly on others, only persons who are morally depraved look out for themselves *by* looking at others, wishing to be like or better than the rest. In the true state of nature, vanity or *amour-propre* did not exist. The self-love and compassion which we shared with all other creatures would there have sufficed to ensure our survival.

Rousseau also supposed, however, that mankind had a unique capacity to change its nature. While every other species of animal has been provided by Nature with the instincts and capacities needed to sustain its life, human beings are by contrast free agents, capable of choice. Unlike animals, always enslaved by their appetites, we are endowed with free will and at least the natural prospect of bearing responsibility for determining how we live. Hobbes had already rejected this ancient conception of liberty, which Rousseau thus resuscitated in distinguishing compulsive from deliberate behaviour. In Hobbes's view, animals were not slaves to their appetites, because those appetites motivated rather than restrained them, he believed, and were consequently the impelling cause of their behaviour and not brakes which thwarted them. He also thought the idea of freedom of the will absurd, since only bodies could be free or obstructed, and the will, being subject to no motion, could suffer no external impediment that would arrest it (*Leviathan*, ch. 21). But Rousseau—on this point indebted to a tradition of classical philosophy which Hobbes had sought to overturn—was convinced that Nature exercised an internal constraint upon animal behaviour, and that our ancestors, because they could always satisfy natural impulses in a variety of ways, would not have been bound by the instincts which impelled and controlled all other creatures (P iii. 141–2, G 148). Every member of our species who was not mentally disabled would originally have been free to govern himself.

He thought it was because men in their natural state were able to *make* themselves distinct from other animals, rather than because they were endowed with any specific or distinctive attributes from the beginning, that our forebears must always have had an advantage over every other type of creature. Pufendorf had supposed that men's physical weakness and timidity must have originally drawn them together, thereby contradicting Hobbes's conception of a natural state of war. Rousseau, however, supposed Pufendorf's conjecture to be as mistaken as that of Hobbes. Human society had not been necessary to avert war or overcome helplessness; its establishment had merely been possible because of free will and the human but not animal capacity to make choices, he thought. It had been optional instead of necessary, arising from human nature's indeterminacy rather than naturally prescribed. Our forebears must have been able to decide for themselves, even in the state of nature, how best to contend with each situation. Their flexible diet could comprise either fruit or meat; they could run with terrestrial animals but at the same time also climb trees; and they could select to confront or flee from danger (P iii. 134–7, G

141–3). In the *Discourse on Inequality*, Rousseau remarks of savage man that it is 'particularly in his consciousness of this liberty that the spirituality of his soul is displayed' (P iii. 142, G 148).

The human race must always have been distinct from other species in still another way, moreover, since we alone possess the attribute of *perfectibility*, a term here introduced by Rousseau to the philosophy of history and the history of political thought. In his original condition each person must have had the capacity not only to change his essential qualities but also to improve them. Once having adopted habits which no other animals could share, it would have been in his power to make those habits a permanent feature of his character, and, in Rousseau's view, it was precisely because men were able to make themselves progressively more perfect as moral agents rather than just different from other creatures that they could undergo a *history* of change. After a thousand years every animal apart from man is marked by the same instincts and patterns of life as the first generation, he writes (P iii. 142, G 148–9), thus anticipating the biological thesis that phylogeny recapitulates ontogeny. Man, however, because he possesses the faculty of self-improvement, is capable of perfecting his nature and likewise is distinct from animals in having what is, in effect, the same capacity to make retrograde steps leading to his self-impairment.

Rousseau thus concludes that our inchoate and latent attributes of liberty and perfectibility had made possible the historical evolution of the human race. Supposing that by nature we must have been very much more *like* animals than Hobbes, Pufendorf, and Locke had perceived, he also maintains that the difference between savage and civilized man is in many respects greater than the difference between savages and other animals (P iii. 139, G 146)— a proposition he pursues at length in a manner that contrasts with the ideas on this subject elaborated by Buffon in his monumental *Natural History*, which had begun to appear in 1749. In the *Discourse on Inequality*, Rousseau lavishes praise on this masterpiece of both science and literature, drawing from it many themes which inspired him about the history of organic life, about the individual identity of species as a whole, and especially about patterns of development in Nature. No other work receives such bountiful attention from him, nor did Rousseau admire any of his contemporaries more than Buffon. The second *Discourse* was actually conceived in large measure as a set of conjectures in terms of human and civil history, similar to the account, in terms of natural history, which Buffon provides of the origins of the earth and the birth, growth, and decay of animals (P iii. 195–6, G 200–1).

Rousseau nevertheless takes issue with Buffon at just the point where natural and human history might appear to converge, and he does so principally by adopting a perspective on our species' mutability which he finds so congenial in Buffon's description of other creatures, but which Buffon himself declined to extend to the study of man. According to Buffon, especially in the second, third, and fourth volumes of his *Natural History*, Nature had established an unbridgeable gulf between the animal and human realms, a qualitative break in the chain of being or *scala naturae* which ensured mankind's superiority over all other animals, on account of our possessing a mind or soul. In 1766, following mainly Edward Tyson, the seventeenth-century English anatomist, he was to develop this thesis with respect to the chimpanzee, which he and Tyson both termed an *orang-utan* (a Malay expression meaning 'man of the woods') that was to serve as a generic name for most of the great apes, until these African and Asian species, respectively, came to be properly distinguished in the 1770s. While allowing that the orang-utan greatly resembles us physically in its outward form, Tyson and Buffon insisted that it could not be a species of mankind, since the animal plainly lacks the human faculties of reason and speech. Rousseau, however, even in concurring that man's nature is uniquely spiritual, disputes both Buffon's thesis and its application to orang-utans in his second *Discourse*, claiming that the diversity of types of men throughout the world suggests that over a long period of development our species might have undergone even more dramatic metamorphoses from its 'first embryo' than those which were due to contemporary variations of climate or diet (P iii. 134, 141–2, 208; G 141, 148–9, 214–15).

Since language was no more natural to man than the faculty of reason it articulated, we could not, as Tyson had done and Buffon would do likewise, point to the languages of civilized peoples as proof of the subhumanity of orang-utans. This mistake, as Rousseau

45

envisaged it, is much the same as that of Hobbes, Pufendorf, Locke, and Condillac in wrongly stipulating that a manifest quality of complex behaviour in society is evidence of human nature. Whether orang-utans were proto-humans or of another species, Rousseau claims, could only be established by experiment, which, following Buffon's own definition of a viable species, meant testing for the fecundity of the progeny, if any, of the sexual union of a man or woman with such a creature (P iii. 211, G 217–18). Monkeys clearly were not members of our race, largely because they lack our human faculty of perfectibility, he suggests. But as he makes plain in a reply to the naturalist Charles Bonnet, who had criticized him on just this point, he thought it at least conceivable that orang-utans possessed it (P iii. 211, 234; G 217, 235).

Rousseau never subscribed to any view of the transformation of one species into another, such as would become central to the Darwinian account of natural evolution more than a century after the publication of the *Discourse on Inequality*. He was too much persuaded of the fixity of species in the chain of being created by God, and in supposing the orang-utan to be a possible variety of primitive man he assumed that this creature walked upright and was shaped much like the rest of us, zoologically distinct from apes and monkeys. His point about such animals is really focused on language, and against Buffon and other natural historians and anatomists he merely wished to stress that, since languages express social conventions and have to be learnt, we must not regard creatures which resemble us physically but lack our command of articulate speech as belonging for that reason alone to a quite distinct species (P iii. 209–12, G 215–18). In his reflections on orang-utans, however, Rousseau was to exercise some influence upon the early history of physical anthropology and evolutionary biology, for his supposition that apparently distinct species might be genetically similar or even identical opened the prospect of a sequential relation of links in the chain of being which would eventually supplant his own idea of fixity and replace it with that of metamorphosis and transformation. No one in the eighteenth century envisaged human nature as more subject to change in the course of its development. No one supposed savage man so much more like an animal than like civilized man. No one before Rousseau came closer to conceiving human history as mankind's descent from an ape. His entirely speculative portrait of the orangutan as a kind of speechless savage in the state of nature happens, moreover, to have been coincidentally drawn with greater empirical accuracy than any description of that animal's behaviour for at least the next two hundred years—that is, until the fieldwork undertaken in Southeast Asia since the late 1960s by Biruté Galdikas, John MacKinnon, and Peter Rodman. In remarking upon these creatures' nomadic existence, vegetarian diet, infrequent sexual relations, and for the most part solitary and indolent lives, Rousseau rather highlights the social gulf which separates us from certain apes, whose biological similarities to us, including above all the composition of their genes, fail to mask great differences of behavioural traits. In portraying human nature stripped from society as rather like that of the most independent ape, his conjectures on the zoological limits of our species point as much to the complexity of the social dimension of our lives as to the simplicity of our original state.

Of course the perfectibility of primitive men in their natural condition had not ensured their moral advance, for the *real* development of that attribute depended upon the actual choices which individuals must have made in adopting their various societal and political institutions. Human perfectibility ensured only that there could be cumulative change in one direction or another, and it was as much in accord with the history of man's degradation as it would have been compatible with the history of his progress. According to Rousseau, man had in fact misapplied his freedom upon those traits which he shared with all other creatures, so that in the course of his development he had suppressed his compassion and self-love and had thus brought about his own corruption. As they had grown gradually less dependent upon Nature, savage men had equally made themselves increasingly dependent on each other, with the original perfectibility of every person exercised in such a way as to conflict with his natural liberty, following his election in society to become a slave to new compulsions he imposed upon himself. The perfection of the individual had in reality produced 'the decrepitude of the species', Rousseau concludes, with our faculty of perfectibility therefore proving the source of all human misfortunes (P iii. 142, 171; G 148–9, 177). It was the abuse of this capacity for self-improvement,

47

rather than natural law, which had made possible the transformation of our merely physical into our significant moral differences and had therefore played the most major role in the establishment of social inequality.

If Nature created the first, insignificant, distinctions between savages, it was chance that must initially have drawn them together. In several passages of the second *Discourse*, as well as in the ninth chapter of his *Essay on the Origin of Languages*, Rousseau conjectures that accidents and natural catastrophes such as floods, volcanic eruptions, or earthquakes must originally have brought isolated savages into territorial proximity, perhaps through the formation of islands (P iii. 162, 168–9; G 168, 174–5, 267–8). Living more closely together, our forebears would have ceased to be nomadic, and in making huts and other shelters out of implements which they would thus have had occasion to invent, they would have begun to settle and form families, thereby inaugurating the epoch of human history's first revolution, introducing with it an incipient idea of property, he claims (P iii. 167–9, G 173–5), rather along lines later to be pursued at length by Engels in his *Origin of the Family, Private Property and the State*. But supposing that this had been the case, Rousseau was convinced that such a revolution in savage men's mode of life could scarcely have brought about the development of social inequality itself, if only because the forces which originally impelled us towards one another, he observes in chapter 2 of the *Essay*, could not be the same as those which must later have driven us apart (G 245). The moral distinctions prevalent in society were established by men themselves rather than by Nature or chance, and social inequality could not have been produced merely by our living in proximity to one another.

It most probably arose, Rousseau suggests, from the way in which savages undertook to *identify* their neighbours, whom they had begun to meet with unaccustomed frequency. When, in their primitive settlements, our ancestors would have come to confront the same persons day after day, they must have begun to take some notice of those qualities which distinguished them from one another. They must have come gradually to recognize those among them who were the strongest, most dextrous, most eloquent, or most handsome, for instance, and in general they would have begun to perceive the differences in their constitution which were due to Nature. Each man, equally, must have come to identify himself in the light of qualities which others appeared to recognize as expressive of his own behaviour. He must have begun to compare himself to persons who were becoming more familiar to him, and he must have begun to attach some significance to the differences that he perceived. In this ascription of value to certain characteristics above others, our ancestors would have transformed their natural variations into moral distinctions. They would have turned their attention upon the talents of their neighbours and also wished to be admired for their own skills. They would have come to envy or despise those persons with traits that were unlike the qualities they possessed themselves, and the unequal distribution of public esteem would thus have begun to set them apart in social hierarchies. While 'the savage lives within himself, sociable man, always outside himself, can only live in the opinion of others' (P iii. 193, G 199). In their interpersonal classifications of the attributes by which they identified their neighbours, primitive men must have transformed a cardinal system of distinguishing natural attributes into an ordinal system for ranking moral preferences, with the 'fermentation caused by these new leavens', Rousseau writes, 'producing combinations fatal to innocence and happiness' (P iii. 169–70, G 175).

Of course the various human traits that were esteemed by our savage forebears could not have made their appearance all at the same time. Our ancestors must have recognized those individuals among them who possessed the greatest strength (a physical attribute) before they came to judge which ones were the most handsome or eloquent (manifestly social attributes, depending on taste), and from Rousseau's account it is hardly obvious why individuals should have found some personal qualities to be more worthy of respect than others. But he was convinced that as soon as men began to attach importance to their differences they must thereby have begun to form their social institutions. In particular, the dexterity and eloquence of primitive men to which Rousseau refers in the first of these passages from the second part of the *Discourse* must have made possible the establishment of private property. For in finding people simple enough to believe his claim that the plot of land he had enclosed belonged to him, the real founder of

civil society must have applied his dexterity upon the soil and his eloquence upon his neighbours in such a way as to render legitimate the most fundamental of all the determinate relations which bind us to one another.

After the establishment of private property, the arts of metallurgy and agriculture must have been developed so as to enhance the productivity of the soil and at the same time increase the moral differences between the men who owned it and those who did not. While poets recount that it was gold and silver which first civilized man, Rousseau, here describing human history's second great revolution, instead follows philosophers who claim that it must have turned round the cultivation of corn and excavation of iron, such as had already made Europeans slaves to new needs but had not yet ruined savage America (P iii. 171–2, G 177–8). In the *Essay on the Origin of Languages*, which embraces a somewhat different view of primitive society in its ninth chapter, he ignores this account of two great revolutions in man's early history, preferring, in the manner of Turgot and the mainly Scottish conjectural historians of his day, to comment on the hunting, pastoral, and agrarian stages of our development, to which correspond the savage, barbarian, and civil man respectively, he remarks (G 265–6). But there is no specific mention of Pufendorf, Condillac, or Buffon anywhere in the *Essay*, nor does that work pursue the inversion of the order of Hobbes's and Locke's doctrines so central to his argument in the second *Discourse*. There, he claims, when with inheritances and the growth of population all the perceptibly available land came to fall under titles of ownership, no person could acquire or increase his property except at the expense of others. The state of civil society must in consequence have given rise to war, placing the rich among our ancestors in even greater jeopardy than the poor, since they risked not only their lives but also their property. They would therefore have had a particularly strong incentive to negotiate an apparently calming peace prescribed by law and enforced by police powers. For the protection of their lives, the poor would have renounced their rights to any share of the property of the rich, so that the dextrous and eloquent members of society, akin to the 'industrious and rational' persons described by Locke in the fifth chapter of his *Second Treatise of Government*, would thus have made their wealth entirely secure from others in the perpetration of a hoax which 'converted clever usurpation into unalterable right' (P iii. 176–8, G 182–4). If the jurisprudential philosophers had proved wrong about human nature, they had nevertheless been fairly accurate in their descriptions of human history, allowing that Locke's conception of private property must have preceded, and indeed been the principal cause of, Hobbes's state of war.

The distinct forms of government which men must originally have adopted—monarchy, aristocracy, and even democracy—would all have owed their origin, Rousseau suggests, to the differing degrees of inequality prevalent at the time of their institution (P iii. 186, G 192). But since each type of government would have been devised to legitimate and give authority to our moral distinctions, it must in every case have followed the same pattern of development. It must have progressively extended the dominion of the rich and at the same time increased the obligations of the poor, until the predominant relations between men in society would have been transformed into those of masters and their slaves. The institutions which at first would have been established by consent would eventually have given way to arbitrary power, and governments must in due course have become so burdensome to their subjects that they could no longer maintain the peace they had been set up to secure. Civil society would therefore have succumbed to revolutionary change, and men must have escaped the periodic crises of their political development only by turning to new masters whose perverse eloquence would have persuaded them to adopt still further principles of slavery and despotism, framed in the midst of disorder and revolution (P iii. 187,190–1; G 193, 196). 'Thereby', writes Rousseau near the end of his work, 'comes the last term of inequality, the extreme point that closes the circle' (P iii. 191, G 197). A new state of nature is established where the strongest predominate—a state of nature not in its first purity, however, but rather one based on excessive corruption.

This sketch of the revolutionary stages of our social history which must at first have produced and then subsequently destroyed the rule of despots was later to be described by Engels in *Anti-Dühring* as a 'negation of the negation' and hence a dialectical interpretation of human history which foreshadowed that of Marx. To be sure, Marx himself never concurred with this judgement and preferred, like Hegel, to read Rousseau as a philosopher of the Enlightenment committed to the abstract natural rights of man, whose realization in the course of the French Revolution marked the political triumph of the bourgeoisie. But if he had read the *Discourse on Inequality* with the attention Engels paid to the second part in particular, he might have recognized a theory of the development of private property and social inequality remarkably akin to his own conception of history as a succession of class struggles tempered by an ideological rule of law. Never again was Rousseau to be so Marxist in his interpretation of society as in the concluding pages of his second *Discourse*.

It should be borne in mind, however, that, unlike Marx, Rousseau conceived his argument as a *speculative* account of the origins of inequality. His ideas were designed to provide not so much a history of mankind as a theory of human nature, and his description of the past was drawn from his understanding of the moral condition into which our species had fallen. The essential qualities of our nature, he believed, could be uncovered only if it were possible to envisage them apart from the contemporary and superfluous features of our conduct, so that the natural man must be stripped away from the citizen, rather than the civilized man formed from the savage. Since he began his enquiry from the perspective of man's present state, it followed that Rousseau's own hypothetical reconstruction of the past owed little to any chronicle of actual events. All facts were to be laid aside, he remarks (P iii. 132–3, 162; G 139, 168), as they do not affect the question. His investigations were hypothetical rather than historical, calculated to explain the nature of things, but not to ascertain their actual origin. His state of nature was thus constructed as a fictitious world from which the corrupt features of society had been removed, and his starting-point was not the remote past, about which little information has survived anyway, but the present world we all know well. The *Discourse on Inequality* was conceived less as a general history of the human race than as a theory of human nature presented in the form of history, and the solitary savages whom Rousseau describes as the progenitors of modern man were no more likely to be found among primitive peoples of the distant past than were the thoroughly modern beings of Hobbes, Pufendorf, and Locke. Rousseau believed that there had never been a truly natural man, but it was only with reference to such a figure that we were able to provide a theory of our moral change (P iii. 123, G 130).

Of course, if the state of nature is a fiction, it follows that there will be no point in our attempting to return to it, as Rousseau himself insists in the longest footnote of his text (P iii. 202–8, G 207–14). 'Human nature never makes a retrograde step', he would maintain later in his *Dialogues* about himself (P i. 935). Once forsaken, our lost innocence can no longer be regained. Even that form of primitive society which must have arisen in what he terms 'the happiest and most stable of epochs' (P iii. 171, G 176–7) was one which civilized man could never hope to recover. Such a bucolic state in which our ancestors would have lived simply and at peace with one another was located somewhere between a past that was imaginary and a present that was real, and it contains some elements of both. If men had ever lived in that condition it would perhaps have been to their advantage to remain there, but a world that had been lost could never be recovered, and a state which was abstracted from the present did not provide the moral principles appropriate to generations still to come. As had already been made plain in his reply to the attack of his first *Discourse* by King Stanislaw, in attempting to return to our natural state we should only plunge into an abysmal world of barbarism and destruction. The ills of corrupt society could not be expunged by adopting the pretence of ignorance.

It was in this fashion that Rousseau employed some of the political imperatives of Hobbes, Pufendorf, and Locke in his own discussion of the origins of inequality. He believed that their ideas provided a quite accurate account, not of our true obligations, but rather of our past as it must have been, and the contractual ties which figured in the theories of each of these and other thinkers helped to explain how men could have entered into those agreements which had made them morally corrupt. Yet since the social conventions whch had depraved mankind were imposed by individuals upon themselves, it had never ceased to be possible, even in corrupt societies, for them to establish institutions of an altogether different sort, Rousseau believed. If our natural liberty had been lost beyond recovery, our capacity for self-improvement, on the other hand, remained intact, and, as would be claimed in the

Social Contract (iii. 12), what is possible in our moral affairs is less sharply circumscribed than might be supposed. Man must have misapplied his perfectibility in such a way as to restrict his freedom when he adopted the institution of private property and passed from savagery into civilization. But if he was perfectible by nature, then the mistakes he must have committed could at least in principle be corrected and overcome. In antiquity civil societies had been shaped within a framework that rendered citizens morally free and politically equal under law; and in the *Social Contract* Rousseau was to turn his attention to the manner in which alternative institutions that enshrined such liberty and equality had been and perhaps even might still be established.

4 Liberty, Virtue, and Citizenship

By the early 1750s, mainly through his first and second *Discourse* and his *Letter on French Music*, Rousseau had won renown throughout Europe as a critic of both enlightenment and civil society. His writings on these subjects did not endear him to those luminaries of his day who had hoped to enlist his support in their campaigns against religious idolatry and political injustice, and Voltaire, already the leading proponent of cosmopolitan culture, decried Rousseau's apparently retrograde endeavour to promote barbarism. In 1756 in the *Edinburgh Review*, moreover, Adam Smith, who was to become the eighteenth century's principal advocate of commercial society, and of the morally refining institutions associated with it, also took a dim view of the preference for savagery over civilization expressed particularly in the second *Discourse*. Together with other *philosophes*, Voltaire and Smith elaborated educational, political, and economic programmes which encouraged mankind's moral improvement, while Rousseau, in fomenting opposition from such quarters, came to seem an enemy of progress in all its forms. Yet as Smith remarked in his comments on the second *Discourse*, its author had dedicated this work to the Republic of Geneva and had acknowledged the profound sense of honour which citizenship of that state had bestowed on him. Rousseau had proclaimed his civic and republican identity on the title-page of his first *Discourse* as well, and, although he was later to complain that his compatriots had betrayed the ideals of their constitution, he was to remain proud of his origins, and of the city which had fired his first enthusiasms, even after his doctrines came to be denounced as seditious by some of his fellow-countrymen.

More than any other major figure of the eighteenth century, he subscribed to a view of the link between politics and morality drawn from classical Greece. If the vices of modern Venetians were attributable to the corruption of their state, the depravity of other peoples was likewise largely due to political crimes and oppression, he supposed, and in his earlier writings he had attempted to trace the lineages of that decadence over wider and more historically remote periods by way of philosophical abstraction from current iniquity. He was convinced that since the plight of modern men under most contemporary governments had been politically manufactured, then states subscribing to alternative political principles could by contrast engender better conduct, giving rise to virtue in place of vice. In his *Social Contract*, published in the spring of 1762, Rousseau was accordingly to draw an uplifting scenario of political association utterly distinct in its character from his account of civil society in his first two *Discourses*. Indeed, the *Social Contract* seems to pursue the central theme of the *Discourse on Inequality* in reverse, in portraying a pact of association which draws citizens together instead of driving them apart, and in safeguarding egalitarian ideals of public engagement which enhance rather than destroy their liberty. Having already depicted the stages of mankind's moral corruption in civil society, Rousseau was now to offer a prescriptive inversion of his earlier argument, by mapping out the institutions necessary for citizens to gain their freedom. In laying the constitutional foundations of legitimate political authority in diverse forms, appropriate to different circumstances, the Republic of Geneva's proudest citizen could thus both decry the predominantly monarchical despotisms of his day while also offering a blueprint for states in which political grace or virtue might be won through their subjects coming collectively to rule themselves.

The most famous line of the *Social Contract*, and perhaps the most often-cited statement from all his works, appears at the beginning of the first chapter of book i, following three brief introductory paragraphs in which Rousseau establishes his authority to speak on matters of right, justice, and utility, not because he is a prince or legislator, but because he is the native son or citizen of a free state and hence a member of its sovereign. 'Man was born free, and he is everywhere in chains', Rousseau remarks, almost as if to recapitulate the dreadful saga of our political metamorphosis already recounted in the *Discourse on Inequality*. The early chapters of the *Social Contract* actually pursue themes very similar to those lying at the heart of the second *Discourse*, in that they attempt to show once again that there can be no natural foundation for civil society, either in the family or in any supposed right of brute force. Force creates no right, Rousseau contends, much as he had claimed earlier that our physical differences provide no warrant for our moral inequalities. If force were to create right, then what is right would be as transient as every change in the disposition of force, and disobedience would become legitimate as soon as sufficient power were acquired. Hobbes had contended in chapters 5 and 6 of *De cive*, chapter 18 of *Leviathan*, and elsewhere that force and right must always accompany one another, since 'words' (that is, laws) without the 'sword' (that is, the means to enforce them) were insufficiently binding. But in the *Social Contract* Rousseau reiterates a distinction between power and authority (in Latin, *potestas* and *auctoritas*) which had meant precious little to Hobbes but much to the citizens of the Roman Republic.

His restatement of the dichotomy between nature and morality in the *Social Contract* also drew him to deny that family ties served as the model of relations between citizens in the state. Two thousand years earlier, in the first book of his *Politics*, Aristotle had already remarked upon the distinction between the inegalitarian bonds holding together members of the family and the fundamental equality between subjects and rulers in a political—and therefore voluntary—association, and Rousseau, both in the *Social Contract* and most especially in the opening pages of his *Discourse on Political Economy*, acknowledges his profound debt to Aristotle on this subject and largely rephrases what Aristotle had already said. Indeed, his contrast between the public and private domains in his *Discourse on Political Economy* also closely follows the distinction Locke had drawn, in the *Second Treatise of Government*, between political and paternal authority; like Locke, Rousseau at first develops his own dichotomy in order to refute what he terms 'the detestable system' of Sir Robert Filmer's *Patriarcha*, which Aristotle had, by anticipation, rejected as well, he claims (P iii. 244). With both Aristotle and Locke, Rousseau shared the belief that legitimate government among persons morally equal to one another was established by consent rather than acquired naturally, and in the *Social Contract*, no less than in his earlier political writings, he was adamant that the authority of man over man in civil society—whether for good or evil—had been and ought to be established by choice and not necessity.

In his work's second and third chapters these venerable ideas are expressed in a new idiom and thus given fresh impetus, through Rousseau's subversive attempt to refute the logic of the whole social contract tradition before him, as he understood it. The philosophy of Grotius in particular now draws his wrath, much as Hobbes, Pufendorf, and Locke had done in his second *Discourse*. While allowing that it was the agreement of subjects which marked the proper foundation of political authority, Grotius, following Cicero and other ancient authors, had argued, in his *De jure belli ac pacis* (i. 3, §§ 8 and 12) dating from 1625, that a whole people could consent to obey a king in the same manner that an individual might freely enslave himself—that is, by alienating or transferring its freedom in perpetuity to a master. Not only Grotius, but Hobbes and Pufendorf as well, had advanced the thesis that the voluntary subjection of individuals or a people to their ruler marked a state's legitimate establishment, in licensing or authorizing its subjects' obedience to an absolute power by way of an irreversible transfer of right. Although the sovereign's authority was unlimited, claimed Hobbes, he or it was only an agent, a lieutenant or representative, of the people's will, an actor impersonating his subjects, who were accordingly the real authors of every performance in their name (*Leviathan*, ch. 16).

Rousseau understood this idea of voluntary subjection to be the corner-stone of modern jurisprudence, and having condemned its iniquitous consequences and misconceived notions of human nature in the *Discourse on Inequality*, he was now, in the *Social Contract*, to decry its illegitimacy and to propose an entirely distinct account of the consolidation of a state's authority through the collective choice of its members. Grotius and his contractarian successors had committed two principal errors in their philosophies of voluntary subjection, he thought. The first was to confuse a state's pact of association with a pact of submission, presuming the establishment of sovereignty and the institution of government, whose foundation and responsibilities they similarly misconstrued, to be the same. As he was to argue in book iii, chapter 16 of the *Social Contract*, government is not formed by contract, and the indivisible sovereignty of a people may never be passed over to a king. In electing to dedicate his *magnum opus* to King Louis XIII, Grotius had shown no compunction in depriving the people of all their rights, Rousseau contends in an especially venomous flourish at the end of book ii, chapter 2, which implicitly contrasts his own career with that of his illustriously self-serving precursor. Truth does not point the way to riches, he remarks, and the people never makes anyone an ambassador, or a professor, nor does it hand out pensions. Instead of locating the state's legitimate establishment in the act by which a people gives itself to a king, it would have been better if Grotius had identified the act by which a people becomes a people, for in that first convention, Rousseau states, lies 'the true foundation of society' (i. 5).

The second mistake of Grotius which he identifies, similarly committed in turn by Hobbes and Pufendorf, had been to suppose that persons may individually or collectively alienate their liberty in freely subjecting themselves to the will of their ruler. On the contrary, to renounce liberty is to renounce our humanity, Rousseau exclaims, and thus to remove all morality from our conduct. An agreement that establishes, on the one side, absolute authority, and, on the other, unlimited obedience, is meaningless and void, for it derives slavery from liberty and renders its agent in contradiction with himself in the imputed performance of his own will (i. 4). In this critique of voluntary servitude, mainly directed against Grotius, Rousseau follows the argument in chapter 4 of Locke's *Second Treatise* to the effect that a man cannot by his own consent enslave himself to anyone. But his principal source was probably not so much Locke himself as Jean Barbeyrac, the distinguished French Huguenot jurist and editor of the chief political writings of both Grotius and Pufendorf, whom Rousseau also chides in the *Social Contract* for dedicating his work (his translation of Grotius) to a king (George I of England), and accordingly hesitating and equivocating in his statements of principle, so as not to cause offence to a patron. Among the voluminous notes which Barbeyrac had appended to his masterly French edition of Pufendorf's *De jure nature et gentium*, first published in 1706, had been the remark joined to book vii, chapter 8, alluding to Locke's earlier contention, that 'no man may so part with his liberty as to give himself up wholly to an arbitrary power, for this would be to dispose of his own life, of which he is not master'. In his critical reflections in both the *Discourse on Inequality* and the *Social Contract*, Rousseau owes a substantial debt to

Barbeyrac's commentaries on Grotius and Pufendorf, and at least his first acquaintance with Locke seems to have been struck initially through Barbeyrac's annotations to Pufendorf. In the *Social Contract* in particular, he was to develop Barbeyrac's transcription of Locke's own critique of voluntary servitude in order to challenge the very foundations of modern political philosophy as articulated in the seventeenth century, employing its terminology now, so as to ensure, not the people's deliberate resolution to subject themselves to a monarch, but their collective realization of their freedom. Many of Rousseau's ideas of liberty, equality, and sovereignty throughout the *Social Contract* were to be constructed round his introductory skirmish with Grotius, Pufendorf, and Hobbes.

At the heart of that speculative and voluntarist tradition, as Rousseau conceived it, lay the belief that masterless men were naturally in need of a commonwealth for protection. The exercise of untrammelled liberty could only imperil individuals' personal safety, it was claimed, so that in order to obtain the security which they rightly valued above their freedom, men must transfer their rights to an authority thus empowered by law and arms to maintain the peace between them, as well as to keep foreign adversaries at bay. Not only did membership of the state require each person's willing renunciation of his freedom, but in establishing a ruler's artificial superiority over everyone else, it transformed all men's natural equality into political mastery and subjection. In the eighth and ninth chapters of book i of the *Social Contract*, Rousseau attempts to turn these propositions inside out. Our proper passage from the state of nature to the civil state must not suppress true liberty, he contends, but instead realize it in transforming our mere impulse of appetite into obedience to a law we prescribe to ourselves. Neither should it establish hierarchical principles of subjection in overcoming our alleged natural equality. On the contrary, it substitutes an equality that is moral and legitimate for our natural inequality of mere strength or intelligence. The connections Rousseau stipulates between these two principles—liberty and equality—inform most of the *Social Contract*'s central themes.

As he explains in both book i, chapter 8 and book ii, chapter 7, the establishment of the state by common agreement of its subjects produces a remarkable change in man—a metamorphosis which is now described in terms of the superiority it engenders over each person's physical independence, but which in the *Discourse on Inequality* had been portrayed as a fatal step towards vice. In claiming that the abuse of men's new condition so often leads to a plight worse than their original state, Rousseau alludes to the crux of his earlier argument, but he here instead stresses the ennobling and elevating spirit of that change, when the social contract, and therefore the establishment of civil society, is properly undertaken. In return for the natural liberty men might possess in the absence of civil society, they acquire civil and moral liberty, of which the first is described as limited by the general will and the second, in binding persons to obey laws of which each citizen is a joint author, makes them truly their own masters. Having described mankind's original liberty in the *Discourse on Inequality* in terms of free will and the absence of control over us by our animal promptings, Rousseau can only have left attentive readers disconcerted by his new definition of natural liberty, now depicted as slavery to such appetites. Unlike the second *Discourse*, the *Social Contract* hardly refers at all to man's state of nature, and its comments on animals are particularly spare and nothing like so appreciative of their benign qualities as those in the earlier discussion.

But the purpose of Rousseau's argument was now different. He wished to show that men's collective engagement in self-rule could immeasurably increase their freedom beyond that of the mere physical independence of savages in their original state, here described as bound internally by their appetites if not externally by their dependence on others, whereas in the *Discourse on Inequality* he had claimed that primitive men were not ruled by their instincts. In opposition to social contract thinkers before him, Rousseau was to depict men's fundamental pact of association in terms of their fulfilment of ambitions they could not even have entertained without it, so that the liberty to remain free from each other's control, which individuals necessarily renounce, comes to procure another, enhanced, dimension in the very act of its forfeiture, as citizens acquire moral personalities and co-operative interests unimaginable to solitary savages. In contrast with the Hobbesian contention that liberty in the commonwealth consists in the *silence* of laws, whose promulgation by a sovereign consequently curtails the freedom of persons under an obligation to obey them, Rousseau judged that laws and liberty could proceed hand in hand, provided that those who were subject to them also prescribed them, there being no sovereign apart from the people themselves. While for Hobbes liberty is exchanged for authority in men's transfer of their natural rights to their ruler, for Rousseau, provided that citizens rule themselves, liberty is won within the state rather than protected against it.

If liberty is central to his conception of a legitimate state, equality is indispensable for the attainment of liberty, he argues, above all in the ninth chapter of book i and the eleventh chapter of book ii. Just as he condemned the insidious effects of property's unequal distribution in the second *Discourse*, so in the *Social Contract* he objects fiercely to the extremes of wealth and poverty, each equally 'fatal to the common good', he laments, with liberty put up for auction, its buyers accumulating the powers of tyrants, and its sellers renouncing their liberty in order to become tyranny's friends. Perhaps the most tenaciously held theme throughout all of his political writings, and indeed his personal life as well, was Rousseau's anxiety to avert or escape from ties of domination and subservience, which harnessed persons to their respective stations in life, destroying their liberty. Dependence on men, he claims in book ii of *Émile* (P iv. 311, E 85), as distinct from dependence on things, engenders all vices, mutually depraving master and slave alike. Believing that equality was indispensable to freedom, Rousseau remained adamant, however, that it ought not to be pursued for its own sake. Despite the virulence of his critique of private property, he never sought its abolition, as would generations of socialists after him, if only because he imagined that a world shorn of private property could bring the principle of equality into conflict with that of liberty. If individuals were to be prevented from acquiring property through their own labour and initiative, responsibility for their subjection would merely be shifted from the rich to the state, their freedom no less stifled than before. Because he regarded smallholdings of property in land as a manifestation of men's self-reliance, he approved of agrarian republics and in his *Discourse on Political Economy* even observes that 'the foundation of the social compact is property', its first condition demanding that everyone 'be maintained in the peaceful possession of what belongs to him' (P iii. 269–70, H 27). In the *Social Contract* (ii. 11), he holds only that extremes of wealth should be subject to political control, so that no citizen would be rich enough to buy another, nor anyone so poor as to sell himself. It is just because 'the force of circumstance tends always to destroy equality', he concludes, that 'the force of legislation ought always to tend to preserve it'.

More even than with respect to our social and economic relations, Rousseau now stresses the political dimension of equality. Every act of law, he contends, binds all citizens indiscriminately, the sovereign drawing no distinction between the persons who comprise it (ii. 4, 6). 'The first of the laws is to respect the laws', he had already claimed in his *Discourse on Political Economy* (P iii. 249, H 8), adding in the *Social Contract* that each citizen is equally subject to them, because laws as such ignore all particularities and individual differences which receive the attention of government, in executing them, but are never appropriate for consideration by the community as a whole. It may well be his exclusion of any possible individual benefits or harm from the sovereign's enactments that prompted Rousseau to remark of it, in book i, chapter 7, that 'the sovereign, merely by virtue of what it is, is always what it should be', although his meaning in that often-cited passage is obscure. But his attachment to civil equality could not be plainer than in his impassioned insistence upon citizens' equal responsibility as full participants of the legislative assembly which exercises sovereignty in each state (i. 6, ii. 3, iii. 15). Together with modern advocates of participatory democracy who so often turn to him for inspiration, Rousseau supposed that the authority of every sovereign—which like Grotius, Hobbes, and Pufendorf he held must be absolute—was legitimate only if each citizen took a fully active role within it. Herein lies the kernel of his notion of popular sovereignty, whose links especially with his ideal of liberty in the state form the corner-stone of the political doctrine for which he has come to be best remembered since its celebration, as well as vilification, in the course of the French Revolution.

Rousseau's conjunction of both liberty and equality with sovereignty comprises a strikingly original element in his writings, which sets his philosophy apart from the doctrines of Plato, Machiavelli, Montesquieu, and others who, like him, had been concerned with political and not just personal freedom. Prior to the meaning he ascribes to it in the *Social Contract*, the concept of sovereignty had been connected by its interpreters to the idea of force, power, or empire, and it had generally pertained to the dominion of kings over their subjects, however that had been acquired, rather than to citizens' freedom. For both Bodin and Hobbes in particular—the best-known advocates of absolute sovereignty before him—the terms *souveraineté* or *sovereignty*, drawn from the Latin *summa potestas* or *summum imperium*, had defined the prevailing—that is, unequalled—power of the ruler. For Rousseau, by contrast, the idea of sovereignty is essentially a principle of equality, identified with the ruled element, or the subjects themselves, as the supreme authority, and it is connected with the concepts of will or right, as he defines them, rather than force or power—again illustrating the divide between the moral and physical dimensions of human affairs around which his *Discourse on Inequality* had turned and which figures no less conspicuously, albeit with his priorities now inverted, in the *Social Contract*.

By describing the whole populace, comprised of citizens if not of all inhabitants, as sovereign (i. 6 n.), furthermore, Rousseau, so much like Paine after him, sought to entrust the common people of each nation with the ultimate management of their own affairs. He seldom, and in the *Social Contract* never, terms the popular assembly which he envisaged as sovereign a *democracy*, since he regarded democracy as a form not of direct sovereignty but of direct government, which required the people to remain in permanent council to execute and administer public policy, in the manner of full-time civil servants or bureaucrats, thereby rendering the state particularly prone to corruption and civil war (iii. 4). Allowing that the exercise by citizens of their popular sovereignty was most likely in small states, geographically insulated from invasion, whose wealth was distributed more or less equally among persons who cherished their freedom, he suggests that Corsica might be the one country in Europe still well suited for fresh legislation (ii. 10). But even in large states, it was always the people themselves and not their appointed executives who held supreme power, as he attempted to ensure for Poland, by way of frequent elections of mandated delegates to their national Diet, when he came to prepare a constitution for its prospective government. Everywhere that the people were sovereign there must be periodic assemblies which could not be dissolved, he argues in the *Social Contract* (iii. 13), showing in the work's longest chapter on the Roman *comitia* (iv. 4) how such assemblies, from which no citizen could be excluded, confirmed that under their Republic the people of Rome had been truly sovereign, both in law and in fact. The tribunes of that state, entrusted by the populace with their sacred office, never sought to usurp the powers of the people themselves, who could when necessary elect to rule directly by plebiscite, he adds (iii. 15). In the presence of the represented, there can be no representation, for 'the moment the people is lawfully assembled as a sovereign all jurisdiction of the government ceases' (iii. 14). Yet unless citizens fly to their assemblies with enthusiasm in such circumstances, unless each serves his country with his person rather than his purse, the state is lost. No major political thinker before Rousseau had ever shown so much devotion to the idea of collective self-expression or popular self-rule. Although he allowed that the common people could be deceived or misled, he believed that the only possible safeguard against despotism was popular sovereignty itself. Only when the people all took part in legislation could they check the abuse of power which some of them might seek to wield. In pretending to speak on behalf of citizens as their representatives, the sovereign authorities prescribed by Grotius, Hobbes, Pufendorf, and their disciples had appropriated the liberties of the true rulers of each state, whose function they reversed by enacting it themselves as their masters' substitutes, thereby becoming the authors of the people's subjection.

Rousseau had already developed a similar thesis in the context of the arts, when in his *Letter to d'Alembert* of 1758, responding to the proposal of a theatre in Geneva whose establishment he thought would undermine the liberty of his compatriots, he called for public and fraternal festivals of the people as an alternative to the professional spectacle of actors, so that his native republic in its entirety, and not just a single corner of it, might be filled with dramatic processions and performers, such as he had witnessed in his youth. In the ancient world, and particularly among the

Spartans, he claims there (A 133), 'the citizens, constantly assembled, consecrated their whole lives to amusements which were the great business of the state and to games from which they relaxed only for war'. In the modern world, that spirit of public engagement has been lost, and with it the people's freedom. Through the arts, science, and religion, no less than in politics, the people have been numbed and made passive, he believed, displaced from the centre of cultural life and herded into its pits and pews. Transformed from agents of what we do into witnesses of what happens to us, we have been turned into a hushed audience and taught deference and timidity as spectators of a plot of which we were once the central characters. The actors who have assumed our roles, that is, our kings, parliaments, and other heads of state, have all learnt that subjects must be kept apart. 'That is the first maxim of modern politics', Rousseau remarks in the final chapter of his *Essay on the Origin of Languages*, where these ideas are elaborated (G 294). It is perhaps because of the strength of his attraction to what he perceived as an ancient ideal of public engagement that Rousseau believed citizens should be denied all encouragement to place their private ambitions first. Participation in a state's sovereign assembly should be compulsory, he thought— a belief which may inform his contention, in book i, chapter 7 of the *Social Contract*, that 'whoever refuses to obey the general will . . . shall be forced to be free'. The meaning of that chilling remark, which Rousseau's liberal critics have rightly scorned for its potentially sinister implications, is ambiguous, although it appears to embrace the view that the law coerces a state's subjects to act in accordance with their conscience and volition as citizens, and hence their own freedom. Nowhere else throughout his political writings, however, does he seem so inattentive to the distinction, upon which he otherwise insists, between force and right.

The *general will* was Rousseau's term for the exercise of popular sovereignty, which he employed for the first time in his *Discourse on Political Economy* of 1755, published together with Diderot's article on 'Natural Right' ('Droit naturel') in the *Encyclopédie*, where the expression figures as well, and which Rousseau accordingly cites as a cross-reference (P iii. 245, H 2), having seen his friend's text in manuscript. Thanks principally to Malebranche, the term had had a certain currency mainly in French philosophical and theological writings from the mid-seventeenth century, and Diderot was to make use of it in several of his own contributions to the *Encyclopédie*, of which he was also editor. But it was Rousseau, more than any other figure before or after him, who took possession of it and ascribed it with a new, specifically political, meaning of his own. In his *Discourse on Political Economy* he had defined it as the will of the body politic as a whole, serving as the source of its laws and its standard of justice. In the *Social Contract*, he ascribes it both to the public interest or common good which the sovereign of every state ought to promote, and to the individual will of each citizen to achieve that good, often contrary to the same person's particular interest as a man or member of other associations within the state. The threat of factions to the realization of a republic's general will is always great, he argues, citing in evidence (in book ii, chapter 3) a passage from Machiavelli's *History of Florence*. He was therefore adamant that the general will, in its focus upon the common interest, should not be confused with the will of all, which was merely the sum of private and thus necessarily conflicting interests, whose preponderance through the mere counting of votes created unstable coalitions, cabals, and political division. He sometimes suggests that for the general will to be realized at all there should be no sectional associations of any kind in the state, but for the most part he supposes that such factions are inevitable and indeed ought to be multiplied, so that each is rendered as harmless as possible, with the general will not so much excluding as opposing them. Referring to a passage from a work by the Marquis d'Argenson on the government of France which was not to be published until 1764, but which he had also seen in manuscript, Rousseau remarks that 'if there were no different interests, we should hardly be conscious of a common interest, as there would be no resistance to it . . . and politics would cease to be an art' (ii. 3 n.).

Since counting votes was as necessary to establish the general will as the will of all (iv. 2), it is not clear how Rousseau imagined citizens would make that distinction, least of all in the light of his contention that the general will could be computed as the sum of the differences between the will of all's pluses and minuses. But the clash between the general and particular will came to be central to his argument and is most plain in his account of the tension it produces in the mind of each citizen, dividing his judgement of what is beneficial to himself from what is right for the community (i. 7). Rousseau's liberal critics have often decried his notion of the general will for its apparent collectivism, but in the *Social Contract* it appears designed to avert rather than achieve the social indoctrination of individuals. Because we had lost so much of our public spirit, the general will of each person in the contemporary world was much weaker than his particular will, Rousseau believed, and it was to be strengthened and animated, not by every citizen's thoughtless echo of his neighbours in a public assembly, but just the reverse—by all men expressing their own opinions alone, having no communication amongst themselves which might render their separate judgements partial to this or that group interest. John Stuart Mill would later show scant patience for a secret ballot, and Rousseau might well have agreed that the people's deputies, where required, should be expressly accountable at all times to their constituents. But in a referendum, plebiscite, or public assembly of all the citizens, in order to ensure that there are as many votes as individuals, every member of the sovereign must act without regard to the rest, he thought, consulting his own general will as an autonomous agent, thus obeying himself alone. Rousseau's distinction, with respect to international politics, between a state's dimly perceived 'real interest' in establishing a federal peace under international law and its tenaciously held 'apparent interest' in maintaining its absolute independence, had earlier been couched in similar terms in his *Judgement of the abbé de Saint-Pierre's Project for Peace*, drafted around 1756 (P iii. 592–3, H 89–91).

Having elaborated the 'principles of political right' (the *Social Contract*'s subtitle) in books i and ii, he turns next to the application of those principles, reversing his priorities between the physical and moral aspects of the state, in order to address its executive power in place of its legislative authority, government rather than sovereignty, force instead of right, as he makes plain in book iii, chapter 1. Unlike sovereignty, which can never be represented, government—described by Rousseau as an 'intermediary body' between citizens both in their sovereign capacity and as subjects bound by law—is always comprised of the people's representatives. Whereas sovereignty is invariably general in its enactments, the executive power of government is exercised only in particular instances (iii. 1). While sovereignty takes only one form, government depends on circumstances and accordingly takes on different configurations appropriate to peculiar needs. Its institutions are localized, contingent, and specific.

Much the most important factor that determines the nature of governments which states must have is their population, with the more dense requiring the most concentrated government, and the least the most diffuse, following the inverse ratio between government powers, on the one hand, and each citizen's fractional part of sovereignty, on the other, as discussed by Rousseau in the first two chapters of book iii. This rule steers him towards a recapitulation of the ancient classification of governments in terms of the number of their officers or magistrates—that is, of the one, the few, and the many, or monarchy, aristocracy, and democracy (or polity)—most famously described by Aristotle, also in the third book of his *Politics*. Similarly following Aristotle, Rousseau addresses his attention to the class structure of states and to the distribution of wealth most propitious to each form of government, pointing particularly to the equality in rank and fortune best suited to democracy (iii. 4) and to the nobility and intermediary ranks between the prince and subjects of monarchy; in a large state, he suggests, these countervailing forces helped to temper monarchical power, whose condensed vitality might otherwise appear its chief advantage when exercised in the public interest, which Rousseau believed was seldom the case.

Bodin, Bossuet, and other philosophers of royal absolutism had claimed that the cohesion of the state was best preserved under the authority of a uniquely pre-eminent power of a single person, but Rousseau was unconvinced by such assertions, contending, by way of contrast with his idea of sovereignty, that it was a fallacy to assume that 'the prince is everything he should be' (iii. 6). Not only is monarchy in both its elective and hereditary forms specially prone to crises of succession, but it is also subject to venal intrigue and ineptitude, he claims, under the machinations of men of small talent with correspondingly great ambition. In his *Judgement of the abbé de Saint-Pierre's Project for Peace*, he pours scorn as well upon princely schemes of territorial expansion in pursuit of empire and money, commending the wisdom of France's

69

Protestant King Henry IV, by contrast, for his spirited effort to negotiate an international Christian commonwealth at the turn of the sixteenth century. He contends that Saint-Pierre could scarcely hope to repeat that endeavour two hundred years later, however, partly on account of his far slighter skills, but mainly because the continent's diplomatic and military configurations had so much changed that no federative league of European states could now be established except through revolutions (P iii. 595–600, H 94–100). Hobbes had supposed that monarchical government was generally superior to other forms, on account of the identity of public with private interest it secured. Rousseau was nevertheless much more persuaded by Machiavelli's appraisal that 'the people are more prudent and stable, and have a better and wiser judgement, than a prince' (*Discourses*, i. 58). Like Machiavelli, he believed republican government superior to monarchy, and in the *Social Contract* even claims that Machiavelli's *Prince*, in its portrait of truly execrable rule, had been secretly intended as a 'handbook for republicans' (iii. 6), disguising its author's profound love of liberty, which Rousseau shared.

In the light of such strictures, he might appear to have been drawn to democracy as the best form of government, but he was in fact adamant that democracy is equally dangerous, above all because, by its very nature, it invites confusion between a state's sovereign and government. The people who make the law must not themselves execute it, he argues (iii. 4), for that would be to render the sovereign particular and to confuse private and public interest even more insidiously than under monarchical government. 'When this happens', he claims, 'the state is corrupted in its very substance and no reform is possible'. Because of its 'advantage in distinguishing between the sovereign and the government' (iii. 5), Rousseau seems to have been best disposed to aristocracy, or, rather, to elective aristocracy, since he deems natural aristocracy suitable only to primitive peoples and hereditary aristocracy 'the worst of all governments'. Elective aristocracy does not depend upon the honesty and wisdom of every citizen, he argues, and it therefore requires fewer virtues than democratic government. Although it could thrive only when riches were distributed with some evenness and moderation, the fact that strict equality is generally beyond attainment serves it well, enabling the daily administration of public affairs to be entrusted to persons of suitable talent whose independent means permit them to devote all of their time to the state with financial equanimity. Under elective aristocracy, Rousseau supposed, the most upright, intelligent and politically experienced citizens could ensure the state's stability as its highest officers and public servants.

Much the most important fact about all varieties of government, in his view, is their fundamental difference from each nation's sovereign. If the people could not administer their own laws properly in a democracy, neither could their magistrates, monarchical or aristocratic alike, rule in their stead. The threat of government's abuse of powers that belonged only to the people was felt as fiercely by Rousseau as by Locke before him, and it is most characteristically that all too frequent tendency of a government's substitution of its particular will for the general will of the sovereign which he regards as despotism. The people of England is free only during the election of Members of Parliament, he remarks in both book iii, chapter 15 of the *Social Contract* and the seventh chapter of his *Government of Poland*. In perversely entrusting their authority as a legislative sovereign to a corporate body that should merely have served them as their executive power, they showed themselves unfit for the liberty it was their duty to exercise directly themselves. So too, in Geneva, the executive power (the *Petit Conseil*) had come to make itself progressively more dominant by assuming responsibilities that properly belonged to the full assembly of citizens (the *Conseil Général*), even obstructing that sovereign body from meeting. With the executive force of his native state's displacement of the popular will, absolute right was corrupted into unfettered power. 'Where force alone reigns', Rousseau remarks about these developments in his *Letters from the Mountain*, here using the term *democracy* to refer to the sovereign, 'the state is dissolved. That . . . is how all democratic states finally perish' (P iii. 815).

Earlier political thinkers had frequently sought to provide safeguards against threats of despotism by invoking principles of natural law which rulers could transgress only at the peril of their souls or even their lives, risking regicide or revolution. Among Rousseau's contemporaries, Montesquieu elaborated a doctrine of the rule of law, which was to prove profoundly influential in Western

71

liberal thought, that distinguished the authority of monarchs from the caprice of despots in terms of it, and also underpinned his notion, with regard to England, of an independent judiciary. But Rousseau, whose brief stay in England a few years later was to prove as trying to his own independence as he deemed Parliament was to native Englishmen, found Montesquieu's conception of law unconvincing too. Contrary to critics who would later dread the abuse of the powers of sovereignty which he had drawn, he believed that the vigilant exercise of those powers by the people themselves was the only safeguard against despotism. Under the principles of his political philosophy, no force could be exercised against particular persons in any state by the sovereign itself, which was constrained by its nature from implementing its own will. That responsibility belonged to government alone. Liberty was thus to be protected not by virtue of an overarching natural law or an independent judiciary within government, but rather through an infrastructural separation of powers, differently conceived from Montesquieu's perspective, between government and sovereignty.

In book i, chapter 2 of the *Social Contract*, Rousseau charges that Grotius had granted a specious legitimacy to slavery and tyranny, by offering mere fact as proof of right. In book v of *Émile* (P iv. 836, E 458), where he repeats that allegation, he claims that Montesquieu had likewise failed to address the principles of political right, being content instead 'to discuss the positive right of established governments'. Nothing in the world of politics could be more different than fact from right, he insists, thus inaugurating a dispute between philosophers and scientists which has divided his admirers, and others, from the disciples of Grotius and Montesquieu to the present day. But in the *Social Contract* Rousseau was also anxious to address the facts of political life, and his debt to Montesquieu's own manner of explaining those facts is striking. Like Montesquieu he was concerned with the natural history and pathology of governments, and with the manner in which states arise, expand, and dissolve, for 'the body politic', he claims, 'no less than the body of man, begins to die as soon as it is born, and bears within itself the causes of its own destruction' (iii. 10, 11). Following Montesquieu as well, he recognizes the significance of physical factors upon the nature of government and the constitutions of states, remarking, with reference to the fourteenth book of *The Spirit of the Laws*, that 'freedom is not the fruit of every climate', and therefore not within the grasp of all peoples (iii. 8). While stressing how much the morality of persons in civil society could be explained with reference to laws and to political factors, he lays great emphasis as well upon the way in which morality determines positive laws, describing those forces of habit, custom, and belief which are engraved, not on marble or brass but in the hearts of citizens, as a fourth kind of law (in addition to political, civil, and criminal) which is 'the most important of all' (ii. 12). In *Émile*, he commends *The Spirit of the Laws* precisely for its treatment of the relation of manners to government (P iv. 850–1, E 468). Despite their differences, Rousseau was greatly influenced by Montesquieu's account of the moral constraints upon legislation. While contemplating laws as they might be, he was concerned in the *Social Contract*, as his first sentence makes plain, to take men as they are. The facts and standards of politics, though distinct, must also go together, he supposed, in turning his attention to assess what was possible in human affairs, as well as to what was right. Like Montesquieu, he inspects constitutions from below, in the light of the social conventions and popular traditions underpinning them, no less than from above, in terms of first principles.

Rousseau's apparent sensitivity in the *Social Contract* to local customs and national traditions, in conjunction with his attachment there to principles of right, won him admirers throughout Europe, above all, perhaps, in countries struggling against foreign domination, or seeking to preserve an indigenous freedom in the course of civil wars that were prey to external powers. When in 1764 the Corsican patriot Mathieu Buttafoco invited him to be the legislator of a free state which he had already pronounced to be uniquely fit for legislation, and when in 1770 Count Michel Wielhorski called on him to comment upon the Polish Confederation of Bar's efforts to free Poland from the tyranny of Russia, Rousseau responded in each case with enthusiasm. Always anxious that his writings not be thought politically inflammatory, he hesitated to become embroiled in the political struggles of his own native city in the mid-1760s, proving reluctant to lend too zealous support to disappointed radical republicans among his compatriots, who eventually rallied to his defence in opposition to a government which had proscribed his works. 'I have a bold nature, but a timid character', he confessed to his disciple and biographer, Bernardin de Saint-Pierre. Never daring to mount any barricades, like Bakunin, or to steer the fortunes of revolutionary parties from committee-rooms, like Marx, Rousseau declined to embroil himself directly in the political struggles of his day, not least because, as he once remarked in a letter to the Countess of Wartensleben, 'the liberty of the whole of humanity did not justify shedding the blood of a single man' (L 5450). But framing constitutions out of a rich civic imagination that need not be put to political trial was for him quite another, altogether more compelling, matter.

To the Corsicans, in his *Constitutional Project* on their behalf, he advised the promotion of their predominantly agricultural economy for the sake of self-sufficiency rather than superfluities, its land and produce to be shared and enjoyed as equally and as frugally as possible, its public revenues collected in kind or labour rather than cash. To the Poles, whose own love of liberty won his applause, he recommended a scheme of education incorporating games, national bursaries, and exclusively Polish teachers, to enable pupils to become 'children of the state' (P iii. 967), together with a plan of legislation embracing a strict liability to their constituents of the delegates of a unicameral national Diet. Each text refers or alludes to themes Rousseau had already articulated in the *Social Contract*, and *The Government of Poland* in particular draws several contrasts between representative assemblies among the Poles and Englishmen, always to the discredit of the House of Commons, whose expulsion in 1764 even of a blunderhead like John Wilkes, as noted here (P iii. 982), showed yet again how little the people of England were in control of their Parliament.

Neither of these works was to be published or widely circulated in Rousseau's lifetime, and he therefore could not be blamed in any way for France's unfortunate annexation of Corsica (in 1769, the year of Napoleon's birth in Ajaccio) or the first partition of Poland (in 1772), in each case soon after he had launched himself into a constitutional defence of the liberties of their citizens. Nor can there be any good reason to share his own belief, entertained in a particularly dark moment of paranoia, that Corsica had been invaded to discredit him. But perhaps both he and some of his contemporary admirers were mistaken to suppose that his political ideas as a legislator for new states could have no revolutionary implications. Allowing that men must always be taken as they are, he nevertheless contends in the *Social Contract*, just as he had earlier done in the *Discourse on Inequality*, that human nature might be changed. In his chapter on the legislator (ii. 7), he remarks that it was the task of such an extraordinary individual, the true founder of a nation or religion, to transform solitary persons into parts of a much greater whole from which citizens would then receive their very life and being. Among the ancients, Lycurgus, and among the moderns, Calvin, had been such legislators, he suggests, adding the Jews' Moses and the Romans' Numa in his second chapter of *The Government of Poland*. Each of these figures had occupied an exceptional position in the state, seemingly moved by divine inspiration, rather like Plato's philosopher-king or Hegel's world-historical individuals, pointing the ignorant and bewildered towards a new dawn which they could not perceive unaided. Once arrived in the politically promised land, legislators of course would take no further part in its affairs, as Rousseau had already intimated in a *Discourse on the Virtue of Heroes* of 1751 (P ii. 1267), which he had drafted along lines inspired by Cicero's *De beneficiis* for another literary prize, offered by the Academy of Corsica, but then abandoned. The function of legislators was not to exercise empire, but only, by a form of sublime seduction, to promote the apotheosis of both the intellect and public spiritedness of ordinary citizens, he claims. They pretend to be interpreters of the divine word. They persuade without convincing. Their office is neither that of government nor sovereign. But like Prometheus, in his gift of fire to mankind, they make men's moral transfiguration possible. Recast by Nietzsche, who loathed Rousseau, such imagery would assume the appearance not of mere guidance but of creative energy and force, passing into a domain beyond civilization's insipid standards of good and evil.

In the *Social Contract* Rousseau was himself to lend inspiration to would-be legislators of the late eighteenth century. In book iii, chapter 15, he remarks that two institutions, *finance* and *representation*, were unknown to the men of antiquity, who had no terms even to express such ideas. The first, which he calls 'a slavish word', and which he condemns for its modernity as well in both his *Constitution for Corsica* and *Government of Poland*, has given rise to the injunction *donnez de l'argent*—that commanding scourge bred of commercial society, similarly decried in his *Essay on the Origin of Languages*—which prompts citizens to pay taxes and thereby hire troops and deputies so that they may themselves stay at home. The second, arising from the idea of feudal government, through its notion of delegated power as realized in the different orders of the Estates General, and then through the contractual bonds around which Grotius and his followers had framed their ideas of sovereignty, similarly estranges individuals in the modern world from their public duties as members of the state, its common self or corporate identity in the form of a *personne morale* being nothing other than the citizens themselves acting collectively, he claims in book i, chapter 6 and book ii, chapter 4. Civil liberty, as limited only by the general will, and moral liberty, as expressed in citizens' autonomy, or their obedience to laws they prescribe to themselves, are by contrast ancient principles, the first Roman and the second Greek, whose definitions by Rousseau in book i, chapter 8 of the *Social Contract* exclude both finance and representation.

While legislators of antiquity had sought to forge links that would attach citizens to their state and to each other, the laws of modern nations only command deference to authority, displacing our pursuit of freedom from the public to the private domain. Where today, asks Rousseau in his *Letter to d'Alembert*, is the 'concord of citizens'? 'Where is 'public fraternity' (A 133)? In *The Government of Poland*, similarly, he calls upon Polish youth to rekindle the 'spirit of ancient institutions' (the title of this work's second chapter) so as to become accustomed to 'equality' and 'fraternity' (ch. 4: P iii. 966, 968; H 172), as citizens of a truly free state. While liberty had once been linked with equality and fraternity, representation had destroyed fraternity, and finance had laid waste to equality, he believed, so that in the modern world, shorn of its ancient associations, it had in effect come to mean nothing more than the pursuit of private gain.

By thus linking hand in hand the ideas of liberty, equality, and fraternity, Rousseau would appear to have heralded a forthcoming French Revolution, even as he fixed his gaze upon a bygone world.

Much of his own veneration for ancient republican liberty had been stirred by the *Discourses* of Machiavelli, but in his own works that esteem came to be fired by fresh enthusiasm, since, unlike Machiavelli, he supposed that human nature was forever subject to change and, while having been corrupted, could nevertheless still be improved, at least in principle. Let us 'draw from the evil itself the remedy which should heal it', he exclaims in book i, chapter 2 of the *Manuscrit de Genève* (P iii. 288, H 110), adding some years later, in book iii of *Émile*, that 'We are approaching a state of crisis and the age of revolutions'. 'I hold it to be impossible that the great monarchies of Europe still have long to survive' (P iv. 468, E 194). No political exhortation was intended in this claim, which was to be expressed with similar vigour by other figures of his day, who hoped that the civilized world might still avert upheaval. But if Rousseau himself both longed, and at the same time held scant hope, for a wholly changed political future of mankind, the principles of his *Social Contract* would in the course of the French Revolution come to be esteemed as if they formed the Ten Commandments of the new Republic of France. This was recognized by Louis Sébastien Mercier, whose *Rousseau, Considered as one of the First Authors of the Revolution* dates from 1791, as well as by Burke, who in his *Letter to a Member of the National Assembly* of the same year condemned the 'insane Socrates' who had inspired a wholly destructive regeneration of men's moral constitution, and in whose memory the foundries of Paris were then casting their statues, 'with the kettles of their poor and the bells of their churches'. No other political thinker, ancient or modern, was to excite greater enthusiasm among revolutionaries of that period than Rousseau, and in 1794 his remains were to be disinterred from their grave on the Isle of Poplars at Ermenonville and brought to the Paris Panthéon where, with great celebration, he was acclaimed a hero of the nation whose politics, culture, and religion he had loathed above all others—to his eternal torment, furthermore, reburied opposite Voltaire.

In 1762 Rousseau had scant reason to anticipate such canonization. On its appearance his *Social Contract* caused an immediate scandal, its distribution in France was prohibited, and he was obliged to flee the country to escape imprisonment, only to find his way to Geneva barred because of equal public outrage there. Yet it was not his ideas on liberty or sovereignty which then occasioned real disquiet. He was judged a threat to civil order principally because the penultimate chapter of the *Social Contract*, on the civil religion, together with similar ideas in his *Émile*, published at almost exactly the same time, were held to be blasphemous, with his political system thereby deemed criminal and seditious only in consequence of its affront to Christianity.

5 Religion, Education, and Sexuality

In pagan antiquity each state had its own deities, Rousseau re-marks in book iv, chapter 8 of the *Social Contract*, the authority of its gods encompassed by its political frontiers. First the Jews, however, and then the Christians paid homage to a god whose kingdom was not of this earth, and whose temporal ascendancy sometimes failed to match his spiritual predominance, thereby giving rise to disunion in separating the state's theology from its politics. Having spread their faith with their empire, the Romans doubted the indifference to politics professed by other-worldly Christians and, fearing their eventual rebellion, persecuted them. In due course, observes Rousseau, Christians did indeed forsake their humility, and laying claim to God's earthly domains they established the most violent despotism of the modern world. In his own day, political and theological identities had come to be disjointed everywhere, even among the Muslims, so that 'the spirit of Christianity has won completely'. Where clergymen wield cor-porate power, they seek mastery over princes by the regimen their holy orders demand and through their rights of excommunication, while in England and Russia, by contrast, princes have made them-selves masters of the Church, at the risk of equally precarious schism between sacred and temporal pretensions to sovereignty. Alone among Christian authors, Hobbes had recognized such threats to civil peace and had rightly proposed that secular and religious power be placed in the same hands. But he had failed to take account of the perils to his system posed by Christianity, and of the fact that, wherever power is concentrated, the particular interest of a prince will always be upheld by his government more vigorously than the common interest of the state.

Following these reflections on Christianity's subversion of the sacred foundations of civil authority, Rousseau distinguishes three main types of religious belief in its social dimension: religion of the man, religion of the citizen, and religion of the priest. The first, the simple faith of the Gospels, dissolves all allegiance to the state; the second, in joining divine worship to love of the law, makes men credulous and intolerant; and the third, in placing persons under contradictory obligations to priestcraft and princely government, sets individuals at odds with themselves and their neighbours. Each of these cults is harmful to the body politic, he concludes, none more so than the first, wrongly supposed by others to be the best imaginable, because of its shared beliefs and profound piety. In fact, a society of true Christians would be so spiritually perfect that its members would be completely unconcerned with worldly success or failure. Citizens would perform their duties out of obedience, determined only to ensure the salvation of their souls. How could a Christian republic ever confront the patriotic warriors of Sparta or Rome, 'devoured by an ardent love of glory and their country'?, Rousseau asks. How indeed could a genuine republic ever be Christian?, for 'true Christians are made to be slaves', their faith more amenable to tyranny than to the pursuit of the public good.

For the state to draw real strength from its members it must be nurtured by a religion which makes each citizen love his duty without intruding upon his beliefs through canons, sacraments, and dogmas. It must require of its subjects a purely civil profession of faith, prescribed by the sovereign merely to excite a public sentiment of sociability, and its tenets should embrace only the existence of an omnipotent, intelligent, and beneficent divinity, the sanctity of the social contract and the law, and the proscription of intolerance. Since belief is not itself subject to injunction, the sovereign can do no more than banish from its territory all persons whose intolerance of others would inevitably threaten the fabric of society. It may even authorize the capital punishment of individuals who betray their civil oath of allegiance—that is, who lie before the law, and thereby display their willingness to break it and thus to commit acts not of impiety but of sedition, as Rousseau stresses most particularly in his remarks on the same subject, anticipating that passage of the *Social Contract*, in his letter to Voltaire on Providence of 1756 (L 424). Theological intolerance is bound to have sinister political consequences, Rousseau argues, and in a note appended to this chapter, which perhaps out of unaccustomed prudence he tried to suppress, even as his work was being printed, he complains of the threat to the very foundations of the state, by way of its regulation of public offices and private inheritances, posed by clerical control over the civil contract of marriage. The corresponding passage in the *Manuscrit de Genève* is more explicit in its attack upon the intolerance shown to Protestants in France, following the revocation of the Edict of Nantes in 1685 and the enactment of 1724 which commanded the Catholic benediction of Protestant marriages and baptisms. Because Protestants in France cannot marry without repudiating their religion, they are at once tolerated and banned, Rousseau contends there, as if it were official policy that they should both live and die in illegitimate wedlock, with dispossessed bastard children. 'Of all Christian sects the Protestant is the wisest, gentlest, most peaceful and most social', he concludes. It is the only Christian Church which permits the rule of law and the authority of civil powers to prevail (P iii. 344).

In stressing the inappropriateness of Roman Catholicism as a state religion, Rousseau's plea for tolerance in the *Social Contract* bears some resemblance to Locke's *Letter on Toleration* of 1689, although his chapter's emphasis on the politically consolidating ties forged by the legislators of ancient republics owes rather more to Plato's *Laws* and, above all, the *Discourses* of Machiavelli, who had similarly found the civil religion of Rome immeasurably more attractive than Roman Christianity's cult of the City of God. No other modern thinker so impressed Rousseau as did Machiavelli, not only for his love of liberty but also for his incisive understanding of the place of religion in public affairs. Yet at least as striking as their similarity is the main difference between their philosophies of religion, for while Machiavelli approved of religious faith just in so far as it promoted the patriotism of citizens, Rousseau was also passionately concerned with the nature of religious belief. Unlike Machiavelli, he was inspired by the life and example of Jesus, by the Gospels, and by the teachings of at least some of the Apostles. He had been moved by bewilderment and wonder at his place in God's universe, such as had troubled St Augustine, whose *Confessions* his own autobiography would echo in a fresh idiom. If in his grasp of the political effects of religion he was plainly under Machiavelli's influence, in his religious convictions themselves, and in his perception of clerical orders and churches, he was equally a child of the Reformation. In Western Europe's already relatively secular republic of letters, he was almost unique in the intensity of his religious convictions. While he did not believe in mankind's original fall from grace, both his *Discourse on Inequality* and his *Essay on the Origin of Languages*, as well as a number of shorter works, portrayed the manufacture of sin throughout human history along lines which manifestly offered a modern recapitulation of our abandonment of Eden and our construction of Babel in the Book of Genesis, with his remarks on legislators and the creation of new states in the *Social Contract*, *The Government of Poland*, and elsewhere in turn following the Book of Exodus. Like the Christian theologian, Pelagius, he was convinced of the essential goodness of human nature in the form cast by God. Like Abelard, around whose forbidden love for Héloïse he was to shape the most successful French novel of the eighteenth century, he was persuaded of reason's power to comprehend God's meaning. Like Pascal's, his enduring faith through the vicissitudes of a turbulent world was illuminated by a profound inner light.

Unless it was his passion for music, no other subject stirred Rousseau so deeply as his love of God. It forms a constant theme of his writings, from the youthful prayers he drafted around 1739 when under the Catholic influence of Madame de Warens, to the defence of his Protestant faith against his detractors in his *Letters from the Mountain* of 1764, to the natural religion of his *Reveries*, drafted mainly in 1777, near the end of his life, in which he portrays—as if it were like God's—his now completely self-sufficient sense of his own existence (P i. 1047, R 89). No subject is accorded more abundant commentary throughout his voluminous correspondence, and especially in his third letter of 26 January 1762 to the Director of Publications, Malesherbes (L 1650), and in another of 15 January 1769 to Laurent Aymon de Franquières (L 6529), Rousseau celebrates the blissful earnestness of his faith: in the first case by rejoicing in the presence of a divine being whose infinite embrace of the wonders of Nature leaves him in ecstasy; in the second through reflections on the inner sentiment by which men are spontaneously drawn to both God and truth, and on the evil for which we alone are responsible in abusing our faculties. But it is above all in an extended passage of *Émile*, the 'Profession of Faith of the Savoyard Vicar', that Rousseau's conception of God receives its fullest and most eloquent exposition. Already in 1761, at the end of *The New Héloïse*, the heroine of Rousseau's novel, on her deathbed after saving her son from an accidental drowning, had uttered the credo of a woman who had lived 'in Protestant communion, which draws its sole rule from Holy Scripture and from reason' (P ii. 714). Julie's identity was only fictional, however, and she had been licensed by her creator to speak her mind. In *Émile*, her last catechism was to become that of an exiled abbot (modelled after two priests Rousseau had in fact known in his youth), conveyed from the slopes outside a town within sight of the Alps to a young fugitive—presented in the first person in effect by Jean-Jacques to himself, setting an example both to the pupil portrayed within the work and, to all its readers, as its author's Sermon on the Mount.

The 'Profession of Faith' is divided into two halves, punctuated by Rousseau's appearance in his own persona as narrator and tutor to Émile, recalling by way of invention the bedazzlement of his boyhood response to the priest's sublime epiphany, when he had perceived another universe such as he was to glimpse in reality on his way to visit Diderot in the prison of Vincennes. In the first part, he describes the duality of human nature, the inertness of sensation, the necessity of God as the external and ultimate instigator of the motion of all matter and as Supreme Intelligence, the responsibility borne by men alone for evil, and their capacity to attain happiness and virtue. In the second part, he condemns belief in miracles and dogmas, and the intolerant pretensions of sectarian churches to universal authority, through holy writ and mysteries incompatible with reason. The first part, designed to refute the scepticism and materialism of some of the leading *philosophes* of his day, offers Rousseau's account of religion in accordance with Nature; the second part, in assailing the bigotry and superstition above all of Roman Catholicism, sets out his critique of religion conceived as revelation.

In the fourth book of his *Essay concerning Human Understanding* (ch. 3, § 6), Locke had claimed it at least conceivable that God, if He so pleased, could 'superadd' to matter a faculty of thinking, thereby animating insensate particles with the power of thought. In the chapter subsequently devoted to 'Our Knowledge of the Existence of a God' (iv. 10. 10), which in fact anticipates some of Rousseau's own arguments, he insisted that it was impossible for matter of itself ever to give rise to thought, and most of his remarks on the subject were designed to combat claims of the materialists, chiefly Spinozists, of his own day, who had asserted what he denied. But his proposition that through God's will matter might be made to think occasioned numerous rebuttals from theologians and philosophers of the early eighteenth century, most of whom associated this claim with Locke's further suggestion in the same section of his work that the truths of morality and religion do not depend upon the immateriality of the soul. Voltaire had commented upon Locke's argument in his *Philosophical Letters* of 1734, and French materialists of the mid-eighteenth century, including Maupertuis and La Mettrie, drew inspiration from it, some (like Diderot) stressing the inherent irritability or vitality of organic matter, some (like d'Holbach) locating all of reality in the physical world alone, thus deeming spiritual substance, the soul, and even God, illusory. In his *Treatise on Sensations* of 1754, Condillac attempted to construct a theory of the formation of human intelligence from pure sensory experience, while in the article 'Evidence', probably by François Quesnay, published in the sixth volume of the *Encyclopédie* in 1756, a similar argument was pursued to show that sensation gives rise to judgement, and in 1758, in *On Spirit*, which scandalized the Church and provoked even more official outrage than *Émile* would excite later, Helvétius was to make this identification of judgement with sensation the corner-stone of his whole work. Locke's proposition that matter might be made to think, and Helvétius's corollary that judgement is just sensation, together constitute the main focus of criticism and the chief point of departure of Rousseau's proof of the existence of God in his 'Profession of Faith of the Savoyard Vicar'.

Both there (P iv. 584, E 279) and in his subsequent letter to Monsieur de Franquières (P iv. 1136), he denounces the supposition of thinking matter as a 'veritable absurdity', 'whatever Locke says about it'. It is not possible to prompt matter to think, claims the priest, for no motion to which matter is subject can give rise to reflection. Contrary to Helvétius in particular, he asserts that the judgements made by persons do not spring from their sensations, for while objects may impress themselves upon our passive senses, we can have no automatic impressions of the relation between objects. Unless we formed our judgements as agents actively responsible for the interpretation of our experience, we could never make errors or be deceived, since our senses would always represent the truth. The philosophy of Helvétius thus fails to accord us 'the honour of thinking' (P iv. 571–3, E 270–2). The materialists are mistaken because they are deaf to the inner voice which convinces Rousseau that his sense of his own existence cannot be generated by unorganized matter, of its very nature bereft of the power to produce thought, which must spring from a cause that animates itself, a voluntary action or spontaneous expression of will. This, Rousseau's *alter ego* contends, is his first article of faith (P iv. 576, 585; E 273, 280).

He had initially been in that state of doubt demanded by Descartes for the pursuit of truth, he confesses, adrift without rudder or compass in a vast sea of opinions, tossed by tempestuous passions and with scant guidance from philosophers—all in agreement only that they must differ from one another, even professed sceptics tenaciously dogmatic in their destructive criticism (P iv. 567–8, E 267–8). Having found in philosophy more grounds for torment than deliverance from such doubt, he had turned instead to the light within him and to the simple love of truth towards which he would allow his heart to lead him. In that way, he soon discovered that he exists and that he has senses whose cause must be external to him, since he did not summon them up by an act of his own will. He could perceive from his sensations themselves that both their object and source are independent of him, thus bearing witness to the existence of other entities apart from himself. Beholding the matter in motion of which the universe was formed, he had come to grasp that there can be no motion without direction, and no direction without a cause which determines it. Determinate motion points to a will, and will to intelligence. That, states the priest, is his second article of faith. Such will was self-evidently wise and powerful, he contends, suffused in the heavens which revolve, the stones that fall, and the leaves carried by the wind. 'I perceive God everywhere in His works', he claims. 'I sense Him in me' (P iv. 578, 581; E 275, 277).

Knowing nothing of the order of the universe apart from the

necessity of its existence, the priest could nevertheless admire its Creator for His craftsmanship. In inspecting his own mind, moreover, he could behold that his will was independent of his senses, and allowing the equal independence of the will of other persons he could see the disorder of 'evil on earth', as distinct from the harmony of Nature, stemming from it—that is, from men's freedom of action, acceptance of which, states the priest, forms his third article of faith (P iv. 583, 586–7; E 278, 281). Human misconduct springs from free choice and cannot be imputed to Providence, he asserts, for God is good and just (P iv. 593, E 285). To complain that He has failed to prevent us from committing evil is to protest at His implantation of morality in man, for as Rousseau had already observed in his letter to Voltaire of 1756, Providence has made us free so that we may choose the good and refuse the evil. Its making us capable of choice excludes its choosing for us. When we abuse our faculties and commit evil, we perform not God's work but ours. 'Man, seek the author of evil no longer. It is yourself!', exclaims the priest (P iv. 588, E 282), as if transcribing the inscription to the tenth plate of *The New Héloïse*: 'Où veux-tu fuir? Le Phantôme est dans ton cœur' (P ii. 770).

Contrary to Locke, Rousseau's Savoyard vicar insists upon the immateriality of the soul, as well as on its immortality, although he professes ignorance as to whether the wicked suffer eternal damnation, and even indifference to their fate. In consulting nothing more than his inner sentiment, he finds that he can at least make the moral judgements that will determine his own destiny. 'All the evil I ever caused in my life was done out of reflection', Rousseau would later lament in an unfinished letter meant for the Marquis de Mirabeau (L 5792), recalling celebrated lines from Ovid and from Paul to the Romans. 'The little good I achieved I did out of impulse.' In the 'Profession of Faith' and in his letter to Monsieur de Franquières and elsewhere, inspired most particularly by the *Discourse concerning the Being and Attributes of God* (ii. 3) of the English philosopher and theologian Samuel Clarke, he terms that impulse of his nature *conscience*, calling it 'an innate principle of justice' (P iv. 570, 598, 1135; E 269, 289) or the inner voice of the soul, which stands to it in the same relation as does instinct to the body. Conscience! That immortal and celestial voice is an infallible guide to virtue, claims the priest, who blesses God for His gifts but does not pray to Him. What could he ask? Not for the power to do good, with which he had in fact been endowed. Nor to have his work done on his behalf, while he collected the wages for it. Had God not already granted him conscience to love the good, reason to know it, and freedom to choose it (P iv. 605, E 294)?

In the second part of his 'Profession of Faith', which concludes with the vicar's recital of his frustrated ambition to remain a parish priest, and with a plea to the young Rousseau to be sincere and to promote a spirit of humanity among the intolerant, he sets the natural religion to which he subscribes in opposition to dogmatic faith, miracles, and revelation. Confronted by the great spectacle of Nature which addresses our eyes, our heart, our judgement, and our conscience, it seems strange that any other religion should be required at all, he remarks. Yet we are told that revelation was needed to teach men the way God demanded to be served (P iv. 607–8, E 295). In Europe alone, we have three principal religions, of which one accepts a single revelation, the second two, and the third three, each detesting and cursing the other two, with reference to books scarcely intelligible even to the literate, the Jews no long understanding Hebrew, the Christians unable to fathom Hebrew or Greek, and the Turks with no comprehension of Arabic. Yet in each case, what every man is obliged to know is confined to books. Always books! Europe is full of them (P iv. 619–20, E 303). In each case that God's emissaries have taken it upon themselves to interpret His meaning, they have contrived to make Him say whatever they wished themselves, by way of signs and miracles mysterious to others, generally invoked to justify the persecution of heretics. A world miraculously free of miracles would be the greatest miracle of all (P iv. 612, E 298).

When not in pursuit of heretics at home, the purveyors of God's revelations send missionaries to proselytize their faith abroad, menacing all who will not heed them with the prospect of eternal damnation. They have seldom dared to go far enough. What fate awaits the souls of Oriental wives enslaved in a harem? Will they all go to hell as punishment for having been so reclusive (P iv. 622, E 304–5)? Of course the holiness of the Gospel speaks to the priest's heart, he admits. Of course there is a sublime grace in the teachings of Jesus, as noble as the wisdom of Socrates. The life and death of Jesus show him to have been a god. But there is too much in the same Gospel that is incredible, repugnant to reason, and impossible for any sensible man to accept (P iv. 625–7, E 307–8). Let God's word be less mysterious. Did He grant us a faculty of reason only to forbid us its use? May we not serve Him best unaided? 'The God I worship is not a god of shadows' secreted in books, the priest insists (P iv. 614, E 300). Let us close all the books and embrace instead His plain truth, because it is inscribed in all languages, accessible to all men, in the open book of Nature (P iv. 624–5, 306–7). The God of revelations speaks in too many tongues. 'I would rather have heard God Himself. . . . So many men between God and me!' (P iv. 610, E 297).

Rousseau should perhaps have been less surprised than he was that such reflections on the essence of religion and Christianity in the *Social Contract* and *Émile* were not at all welcomed by the Church in France. Voltaire took sufficient care to broadcast his severest censure of Roman Catholicism from the safer side of the French border, but Rousseau wrote with reckless abandon, unprepared for the official response, in the country in which he then resided, to the poetic licence of his exalted images, following the publication of the *Social Contract* in Holland and of *Émile* simultaneously in both Holland and France. His works' proscription in Geneva, preventing his escape to his homeland, filled him with even greater dismay. When in August 1762 the Archbishop of Paris issued a mandate denouncing *Émile*'s pernicious doctrines after the Sorbonne had officially condemned the text and the city's *Parlement* had ordered it to be burnt by the public executioner, Rousseau had already made his escape from France. 'Your only proof against me is to cite original sin', he protests in his reply, which forms the longest of his writings devoted to theology, the *Letter to Christophe de Beaumont*, published early in 1763. How could God have made us innocent merely in order that we should prove sinful and thereby be committed to hell?, he asks. Is the harsh doctrine of original sin not principally an invention of St Augustine and the theologians, rather than the essence of the Scriptures? Do we not both agree that mankind was created good, with you claiming that he is evil because he has been so, and I showing instead how he in fact became evil? Which of us is closest to first principles? *Émile*, Rousseau insists, was intended principally for Christians, cleansed of original sin by baptism, as pure in heart as was Adam when first made by God (P iv. 937–40).

He had hoped to find refuge in Geneva, but when its government, the *Petit Conseil*, burnt both *Émile* and the *Social Contract* in June 1762—for their scandalous impiety and threat to public order as well as religion—he had been obliged to flee, initially to Yverdon, in the territory of Berne, and then to nearby Môtiers, from which he would later be cast out by villagers who stoned his house. At first eager that his compatriots, in their submissions on his behalf, should restore his standing among them, he found the government's supporters, or *Négatifs*, too powerful in their opposition to such *Représentants*, and soon despaired of any political reinstatement of his rights of citizenship, renouncing them himself. When in September 1763 the case against him was put in a collection of *Letters from the Country* by Geneva's Procurator General, Jean-Robert Tronchin, he sought only self-vindication in his response of the following year, his *Letters from the Mountain*. Since Protestantism was tolerant as a matter of principle and, like the civil religion of his *Social Contract*, was dogmatic only in condemning intolerance, how could the *Petit Conseil* of a Protestant state adopt the persecuting ferocity of St Paul and the judicial rigour of the Inquisition? (P iii. 702, 716, 781), he wonders. Rehearsing at some length the history of assemblies of the *Conseil Général*, which had been 'the salvation of the Republic' when it had been threatened by famine, tyrants, and wars (P iii. 856), he now condemns the degeneration of a body politic whose constitution he had found a shining example to the rest of Europe, a beautiful model which his *Social Contract* had been designed to preserve, out of patriotic devotion. Of course, as he had already made plain himself, it is impossible to arrest political decay. By a 'natural progression', the government of Geneva had changed its form, 'passing by degrees from the many to the few', he remarks (P iii. 808–10), as if to anticipate Robert Michels' iron law of oligarchy with a specific illustration. 'Nothing is more free than your legitimate state; nothing more servile than your state as it is', Rousseau concludes (P iii. 813).

These protestations of a loyal citizen's sincere belief were applauded in many quarters in Geneva and elsewhere, and they later came to inspire the young Hegel and other lovers of freedom, similarly drawn to an unmysterious God, manifest in Nature. But they could hardly have endeared Rousseau to the prevailing powers of his day, and both the Archbishop of Paris and the *Petit Conseil* of Geneva rightly perceived *Émile* and the *Social Contract* as threats to every form of established authority. It was all the churches of Christendom that were interposed between Rousseau and God, all the governments of modern states that stood between each people and itself as sovereign. The institutional replacement of both individual will and collective action by forces which deprived persons of their spiritual and civic identity was the principal moral calamity of contemporary civilization, he supposed, for freedom of conscience required an unmediated God no less than did legislative freedom of assembly require an unrepresented sovereign. Obscurantist theology and despotic power together made men dependent on the will of others, and it was therefore the agents of such forces, understanding themselves in the light of his philosophy to have been challenged by Rousseau's pleas for liberty, who were most anxious to suppress them.

To overcome dependence on others and achieve self-reliance, Rousseau maps out a programme of education in *Émile* which has as its central aim the freeing of children from the tyranny of adult expectations, so that their faculties may develop unfettered, each in its good time. Early in the first book, he distinguishes three kinds of education according to their different sources, which he identifies as nature, things, and men. Only the person in whom these forms of discipline all coincide can be well brought up, he remarks, but then notes how difficult such a comprehensive education must prove, since natural man lives entirely for himself, while civil man, who lives for the whole community, must be denatured, his independent identity transformed into a relative existence, rendering him part of a greater whole. Yet if natural or domestic education could somehow be reunited with civil education, he suggests, the contradictions in man might be removed, and with them a major obstacle to human happiness (P iv. 247–51, E 38–41). Some of Rousseau's interpreters came to suppose this reconciliation to be the principal object of *Émile*, which could accordingly be read as a manual for children's development towards citizenship, whose responsibilities are outlined later in the text and are addressed at length in the *Social Contract*. But the short passage in *Émile* which is devoted to the subject of politics, covering some twenty pages towards the end of book v (P iv. 833–52, E 455–69), does not seem to have been intended by Rousseau to crown the meticulously elaborated plan of a domestic upbringing with a sublime education for public life. Although it recapitulates certain themes of the *Discourse on Inequality* and *Social Contract*, it does so more by way of sketching a course of study upon which Émile might later embark than by taking full measure of a political education for which he still remains unready, and the tutor confesses that he would not be surprised if his pupil were to complain that he had built his edifice of wood rather than men (P iv. 849, E 467). Much of *Émile*'s diffuse structure and perhaps overloaded contents, including its somewhat cryptic passage on politics, may have been due to Rousseau's fear, following a period of ill health in the late 1750s, that this would prove to be his last major work. When after its publication he began to draft a sequel, posthumously published as *Emile and Sophie, or The Solitaires* (P iv. 879–924), he portrayed Émile, not as a citizen engaged in public affairs, but as a grown man writing in despair to his tutor that his world had collapsed, his wife had deserted him, and his education had proved unequal to his human failings.

Though Émile's intellectual and moral development is meant to embrace the company of men and women, it does so in a manner which is deliberately unforced and always designed to be compatible with his natural dispositions. It never recasts his character, or prepares him for a new identity as part of a whole greater than himself, in the manner stipulated in Rousseau's account of citizenship and popular sovereignty in the *Social Contract*. On the contrary, it remains faithful to the central theme of the *Moral Letters* which he penned in 1757 for Sophie d'Houdetot, Madame d'Épinay's sister-in-law, with whom he was then infatuated and whom he served as a spiritual confessor and tutor on matters of the heart. Rousseau sketched only six *Moral Letters* for Sophie, largely on the model of the spiritual quest pursued by Descartes in his *Discourse on Method*. But these *Moral Letters*, when enlarged and reassembled, were to be filled out as the text of *Émile*. Addressed to a woman and to her pursuit of felicity, they have little to do with the ordeals and attractions of a civic identity, pointing instead to a sphere of self-reliance and self-sufficiency which concentrates upon the solitary individual. 'Let us begin by becoming ourselves again, by concentrating only on us', Rousseau remarks in the sixth of these letters. Let us seek to know ourselves as we are, to separate ourselves from all that we are not, for that grasp of the human self and of the nature of one's own being points the way to knowledge of mankind (P iv. 1112–13).

This was also to be the guiding thread of Émile's education, according to his own nature, but it is not a central theme of the *Social Contract*. For Rousseau's plan of a civil education, readers must turn elsewhere, especially to his *Discourse on Political Economy* and *The Government of Poland*, both heavily influenced by Plato's *Republic*. In *Émile* itself, he commends the *Republic* as 'the most beautiful treatise on education ever written' (P iv. 250, E 40), although he makes it plain that he has in mind the idea of a public education, and holds that 'noble genius' at fault for the *Republic*'s 'civil promiscuity' in confounding the two sexes in indiscriminate physical exercises, requiring women to be men because, after abandoning private families, Plato no longer knows what their role should be (P iv. 699–700, E 362–3). By contrast with *Émile*, the *Discourse on Political Economy* and *Government of Poland* are crucially concerned with matters of public education, and accordingly they, but not *Émile*, are largely cast in the *Republic*'s image. In the *Discourse on Political Economy*, Rousseau speaks of the art of making men love their duty and the laws, and of teaching citizens to be good by setting examples of civic virtue and patriotism (P iii. 251–2, 254–5; H 10, 14–15). It is there, in the name of a civil education, prescribed by government, that the rearing of the young in the bosom of equality is held to be one of the most important functions of the state, for 'citizens cannot be formed in a day, and in order to have them as men it is necessary to educate them as children', he remarks (P iii. 259–61, H 20–1). It is in chapter 4 of *The Government of Poland* that Rousseau describes the need for infants to see nothing but the fatherland from the moment of their birth, so that their mothers' milk will be laced with an indelible love of their country, from which they will not be steered away until their death (P iii. 966, H 172). It is there that Rousseau speaks of gymnastic exercises performed publicly and in common, with awards for excellence determined by the acclamation of spectators (P iii. 968). References to Plato throughout Rousseau's works are more abundant than to any other authority apart from Plutarch and the Bible, and it is in these passages devoted to a civil education, together with the *Letter to d'Alembert on the Theatre*, that the influence of Plato's *Republic* on his philosophy is most conspicuous.

It is also these texts, as well as the *Letters from the Mountain*, that most plainly exhibit the influence on him of Plato's *Laws*. When in the eighth of his *Letters from the Mountain* he observes that a free people may have leaders but not masters in its obedience to wise laws (P iii. 842), or when in his *Discourse on Political Economy* he speaks of the celestially wonderful work of law to which men owe their justice and liberty (P iii. 248–9, H 6–7), it is to Plato's conception of law that Rousseau is most indebted. The rule of law in his philosophy stands to citizens in much the same way as does God to those who love Him, and the sovereign to its subjects. It is a spiritually ennobling presence whose authority is acknowledged as externally imposed and at the same time is felt most deeply within the human soul. To that essentially Platonic and then subsequently Christian notion of a sacred principle of order which is inwardly binding, Rousseau was to add the dimension of freedom and a vital element of volition that was to form the kernel of his theory of the general will, and from which Kant would draw much inspiration in his idea of autonomy and his moral philosophy as a whole. But in *Émile*, which maps the lineages only of a domestic education, these features of public life and civic engagement form an insignificant part of Rousseau's argument.

Like so many of his major works, *Émile* was conceived in large measure as a rebuttal of alternative views on the same subject. If the section forming the 'Profession of Faith of the Savoyard Vicar' attempts to refute Locke and Helvétius, the whole work's broader argument about education in general similarly confronts the doctrines of these two authors—with respect to Helvétius, once again his *On Spirit*, in the case of Locke, his *Thoughts concerning Education* of 1693. The first page of *Émile*'s preface announces the freshness of the subject which Rousseau is about to address, following Locke's work (P iv. 241, E 33), and thereafter his text abounds with references or allusions to it, none more important than his remark in book ii that 'To reason with children is the great maxim of Locke'. Such instruction, it had been contended in the *Thoughts concerning Education* (§ 81), should only be commensurate with children's capacities, but Rousseau judged the whole of Locke's enterprise of reasoning with children absurd, there being nothing more dangerous than the shaping of immature minds, particularly from birth to puberty, and nothing more stupid than children subjected to the straining logic of rational discourse (P iv. 317, 323; E 89, 93).

'Nature wants children to pass through childhood before they become men', he insists, both in *Émile* and in *The New Héloïse*. 'To know good and evil, and to sense the reason for man's duties, are not a child's affair' (P ii. 562, P iv. 318–19, E 90). Locke had remarked (§ 110) that the habit of liberality could be cultivated among children by so arranging their transactions as to ensure that experience convinces them that the most generous person always comes off best (P iv. 338, E 103). In *Émile*, however, Rousseau makes it plain that from first-hand acquaintance he knew better. Conflating perhaps three different occasions between 1735 and 1742, in Chambéry, Lyons, and Paris, when he had served as a tutor to uncontrollable little tyrants whose capriciousness had rendered his life miserable, he remarks that he had painfully learnt himself that the only way to make a child do what one wishes is to prescribe nothing, forbid nothing, exhort nothing, and avoid boring him with useless lessons (P iv. 364–9, E 121–4). These are rather different injunctions from the earnestly attentive and self-consciously solicitous precepts he had put forward in two memoirs which he drafted as a young man to Jean Bonnot de Mably, the father of one of his horrid pupils and brother of both Mably, the historian, and Condillac (P iv. 1–51); but in middle age, with his own children abandoned and no such fraught responsibilities, he could speak more freely. Locke had thought it sensible to fill a child's room with contrivances that might be used to teach him to read while he imagined that he was only playing, such as by pasting letters on to dice (§§ 148–55). What a pity he had forgotten the child's desire to learn, which, once inspired, could have dispensed with dice, Rousseau exclaims (P iv. 358, E 117). I am 'very far from supposing that children do not reason at all', he adds in book ii. On the contrary, they reason very well in matters pertaining to their immediate and palpable interest. But it is a mistake to make them reason in Locke's fashion about what they cannot understand or what does not touch them in any way, such as their future welfare, their adult happiness, or the esteem in which they will be held. To immature minds lacking foresight, such concerns are alien, insignificant, and unworthy of attention (P iv. 345–6, E 108).

Together with other pedagogues, Locke had of course been right to prescribe exercise for children's bodies, which ought not to be deformed by the tight clothing, belts, and costumes of French modes of dress in particular, so unhealthily constraining, not only for children, but even for grown men. 'Think me all face' was the compelling remark he had attributed to a Scythian philosopher who had gone out naked in the snow, when asked by an Athenian how he could expose anything more than his face to the cold (§ 5). But why, then, would Locke not leave children's feet to suffer the natural hazards of hot temperature (§§ 7, 30)? 'If you want man to be all face', Rousseau suggests he might say in confronting Locke, 'why do you blame me for wanting him to be all feet?' (P iv. 371, 374; E 126, 128). The 'wise Locke', having studied medicine, had also been right to recommend that drugs be administered to children only sparingly (§ 29). But he ought to have pursued his own logic further, and to have recognized that doctors should never be summoned at all unless their patient's life was in danger, for only then could such professional healers do no other damage than to kill him (P iv. 271, E 55).

Although admirable in some details, the whole of Locke's philosophy of education was misconceived, according to Rousseau, because he regarded children as if they were immature adults in journeyman apprenticeships for their maturity, cultivating skills and learning trades which would prepare them for their careers as gentlemen, not least the keeping of accounts (§§ 201–11), at which Locke's own mastery may be unsurpassed among Western civilization's leading thinkers. But to be a true gentleman is to be 'a plaything of public opinion', paying court to flattery, Rousseau suggests, adding, on the opening page of book v, that he 'does not have the honour of raising a gentleman' and will therefore be prudent not to imitate Locke on that point. Almost as if to anticipate Marx in *The German Ideology*, where he complains of men being exclusively hunters, or fishermen, or shepherds, or critics,

Rousseau contends, against Locke, that he does not want his pupil to be an embroiderer, or gilder, or varnisher, nor a musician, actor, or writer, although his aim is mainly to distinguish useful and stimulating trades from corrupt and demeaning ones, rather than to protest, in Marx's fashion, against the enforced division of labour in general (P iv. 471–3, 692; E 196–7, 357). Locke's entire method, so full of superstition, prejudice, and error, Rousseau observes, is to conceive the ultimate end of education first, beginning with a notion of God, a history of the Bible, and generally the spiritual side of human nature, only then passing to the physical (§§ 136–8, 190–2). To form a proper notion of spirit, one must start with bodies, but in his too ethereal philosophy of education, Locke only serves to establish materialism (P iv. 551–2, E 255).

Rousseau was furthermore convinced that, with regard to the subject of domestic education, Helvétius's *On Spirit* formed the most sinister contemporary example of such materialism. In a letter he drafted for Jean-Antoine Comparet in September 1762 (L 2147), and in a note of the first of his *Letters from the Mountain* (P iii. 693, 1585), he claims that he had originally intended to attack this celebrated work but had then discarded his criticisms in order to dissociate himself from the muckrakers which *On Spirit* had aroused. The surviving manuscripts of *Émile* suggest that much of his hostility to Helvétius may have been fomented more by his rereading of the text in the autumn and winter of 1759–60 than by his first acquaintance a year earlier, but, in addition to the manifestly plain allusions to *On Spirit* in the 'Profession of Faith of the Savoyard Vicar', there are express objections to Helvétius's sensualist philosophy in the draft of *Émile* of early 1759, known as the *Manuscrit Favre*, which are missing from the finished text, as well as numerous marginal annotations, to much the same purpose, in his own copy of Helvétius's work (P iv. 113, 344, 1121–30, 1283–4; E 107). All of these passages concentrate on the dictum 'Juger n'est jamais que sentir' or its derivatives, from the opening pages of the first discourse of *On Spirit*, regarded by Rousseau as utterly mistaken in conflating the passive and immediate perception of objects with the actively construed perception of their relations.

In the fifth part of *The New Héloïse*, where he offers the fullest treatment of the subject of education in his mature writings apart from *Émile*, he attacks *On Spirit* as well for its contention that genius is merely a product of circumstance, on the grounds that this presumes our minds are nothing more than pliant clay. By way of an exchange of views between Saint-Preux and Julie, on the one hand, and Julie's husband, Wolmar, on the other, Rousseau puts the contrast between his own philosophy of education and that of Helvétius, as he understood it, in its sharpest form. Wolmar, speaking largely for Helvétius, insists that in the absence of vice or error in Nature, any malformation of men's character can only be due to improper breeding, to which Rousseau himself appends a manuscript note, doubting that the author of *On Spirit*, if he had considered the matter properly, could really have supposed that all persons are mentally indistinguishable at birth and vary only in their upbringing. If differences between us are always due entirely to the effect of education, asserts Saint-Preux, then it would be necessary only to instil in children those qualities which their tutors wished them to possess (P ii. 563–5, 1672). Agreeing with Julie's contention that infancy has its own ways and feelings which must not be precociously accelerated, Saint-Preux holds, contrary to Wolmar, that each infant is born with a character and talents uniquely its own. The dictum 'L'éducation peut tout', which in 1773 would become the title of a chapter of Helvétius's posthumously published *On Man*, and which would also prompt Diderot's objections on slightly different grounds, was for Rousseau incompatible with any proper understanding of the nature of human development, individuality, and freedom.

In *Émile*, no less than through his fictional exchange of *The New Héloïse*, he prescribes the difficult art of governing without precepts and of doing everything by doing nothing (P iv. 362, E 119), which is just the opposite of training minds or improving character. The most important rule of all education is not to gain time but to lose it, to take the unaccustomed path, he informs his readers, to ensure that a child's first education leaves no stamp upon it, but is instead 'purely negative' (P iv. 323–4, E 93–4). A positive education, in the manner of Helvétius, is one which, in his *Letter to Christophe de Beaumont*, Rousseau condemns as an attempt to form young minds before their time, encumbering children with the attributes of men. By contrast, he there describes a 'negative education', once more, as enabling children to embark upon their own development, and as therefore the only kind which is good (P iv. 945). Even in his scheme of public education in *The Government of Poland*, he puts precisely the same proposition yet again. Only a negative education which accords with children's natural dispositions can avert the birth of vice, he claims (P iii. 968). His refutation of Helvétius thus inclines him in *Émile* and elsewhere towards a conception of men's natural attributes as in some respects less plastic, less malleable, than they are depicted in his *Discourse on Inequality*.

In pursuit of a programme of negative education, tutors are advised by Rousseau to set aside books and instead provide lessons from which children may learn through first-hand experience, sometimes in situations so comprehensively engineered in advance as to obscure the sense in which it may be supposed that they have been made dependent upon things but not men, thereby retaining their liberty, as Rousseau defines it in *Émile*. Reading is, by and large, the curse of childhood, he remarks, and even the charming fables of La Fontaine should be avoided, the moral purpose of such poetic tales being useless to children who, as likely as not, fail to understand their meaning and identify with quite the wrong characters within them (P iv. 351–7, E 112–16). Since we are born both physically and spiritually incomplete, we should be allowed to pass naturally through the stages of our own organic growth, from infancy, to childhood, to puberty, to adolescence, and then adulthood—to which the books of *Émile* itself, as a work of natural education, roughly correspond. With life come needs, Rousseau observes in book i (P iv. 272, E 56), but these are not the same as a child's desires, which are so excited by the imagination that they can never be satisfied, rendering him tyrannical in his ambitions and irascible in his frustrations, for reasons which Freudians would later describe as infants' polymorphous perversity. A child will find contentment, not in the limitless extension of his faculties, nor in the curtailment of his desires, but in the diminution of the excess of desire over the strength of his faculties, putting both his will and his power in balance (P iv. 304, 312; E 80, 86).

As his mind and body develop, so do his nascent passions take root. Émile was born not to be solitary but, like all other members of his species, to enter into the moral order or domain of social life (P iv. 522, 654; E 235, 327). Our weakness renders us sociable, Rousseau now suggests in the manner of Pufendorf, our common miseries drawing us together by affection, as our common needs unite us by interest (P iv. 503, E 221). From the gut reactions of pity, the first relative sentiment, will stem children's identification with the suffering of others, in assuming such persons' very being (P iv. 505–6, E 222–3). In book iv, Rousseau accordingly offers his account of pity in three maxims: first, that we put ourselves in the place, not of those who are happier, but of those who are more miserable, than we are; second, that we pity others only for such suffering which we suspect it might be our misfortune to experience as well; and third, that we feel compassion, not for the extent of others' predicament, but for the depth of their unhappiness (P iv. 506–9, E 223–5). In the company initially of adults and then of children like themselves, the young also come to find their cravings satisfied by those who nourish their burgeoning self-esteem, through the impact they make upon them and later their perception of how others see them. Let us extend *amour-propre* to other beings, Rousseau remarks, thereby making the sense of our own potency significant for the persons around us, which we can only manage to do if we are accorded recognition, rendering our natural *amour-propre* a moral virtue. In such terms, strikingly different from his argument in the *Discourse on Inequality*, is the usefulness of *amour-propre* distinguished from pride and vanity, which now appear to be corruptions rather than expressions of it (P iv. 494, 534, 536, 547; E 215, 243–5, 252).

Our exodus from childhood, moreover, is equally prescribed by Nature. In our physical development, we pass progressively from the innocence of still absent desire to the incipient passions of puberty, which, with more conspicuous manifestations of sexual difference, and their mental attribution of importance to it, mark children's second birth (P iv. 489–90, 498; E 211–12, 217). The 'fire of adolescence, far from being an obstacle to education, is the means of consummating and completing it', writes Rousseau in book iv, recommending that tutors answer youthful questions about sex without mystery, embarrassment, or smiles, there being less danger in satisfying a child's sexual curiosity than in exciting it (P iv. 496–7, 520; E 216, 233). The stirring of a fresh passion also prescribes that, if it is to be fully relished, it must be properly channelled, so that, to be loved, a young man finds that he must make himself lovable, his need for sex thereby itself nurturing an interest in friendship (P iv. 494, E 214–15). Here especially, but indeed throughout the whole of the work, its readers are offered images of the endogenous transfiguration of human passions, coming to their fruition with least impediment when unassisted by Émile's tutor. Sublimated by the reciprocal affection of love, the selfish prompting of sexual desire is enriched, Rousseau supposed. Locke, by contrast, after commenting on the benefits of voyages to other countries, had concluded his *Thoughts concerning Education* with his young gentleman at the threshold of marriage, entrusting him thereafter to the attentions of his wife (§§ 212–13, 215). Rousseau also includes a section on travel towards the end of *Émile*, remarking that whoever has seen only one people does not know men (P iv. 827, E 451). But he does not match Locke's coyness about sex and instead devotes part of the fourth and most of his fifth book to the consummation of sex in love, and to the fulfilment of a man and woman in each other.

'Woman is specially made to please man', Rousseau remarks in book v, introducing Émile to the companion, Sophie, whom the tutor has promised him, as if complying, like God, with Adam's need for Eve. Endowed with all the traits that suit the condition of her species and her sex, both physically and morally (P iv. 692–3, E 357–8), she is capricious by disposition, learning through simple devotion also to become religious. But while she is aware of her natural talents, she has had scant opportunity to cultivate them and has been content instead to train her pretty voice to sing tunefully and her pretty feet to walk daintily (P iv. 747, 750–1; E 394, 396). Although, like other women, Sophie is temperamentally more precocious than men, her faculty of judgement having been formed earlier, she is not as well suited as are men by their nature to pursue abstract and speculative truths. Rather than plumb the depths of the sciences of reasoning, women ought to skim them, employing their enhanced powers of observation in place of men's greater genius, attending less to reading than to the world at large, which is 'women's book' (P iv. 736–7, 752, 791; E 386–7, 397, 426). By no means is the fairer sex imperfect, for at birth women are equal to men, and until the age of puberty girls are more or less indistinguishable from boys. But women are constitutionally different from men, and in their sexual development they appear in a sense always to retain their childhood, continually in a natural state albeit not perpetually innocent, their proper purpose being to produce children themselves (P iv. 698–700, E 362–3). Émile's announcement to his tutor, in the final paragraph of Rousseau's work, that Sophie is pregnant heralds not only the father's joy but also the fulfilment of Sophie's own life in particular, with the gestation of a fresh pupil, assumed by Émile himself if not by Rousseau to be a boy, whose care will be entrusted to a new tutor similar to his own (P iv. 867–8, E 480). Sophie, who has a mind that is agreeable but not brilliant, and solid but not profound, is encouraged to perfect just the labours of her sex, which she knows best (P iv. 747–8, E 394–5). Differing from men in both temperament and character, women ought not to partake of the same education, Rousseau concludes (P iv. 700, E 363).

For advocates of women's liberation from the tyranny of men, such reflections have proved as welcome as was the 'Profession of Faith of the Savoyard Vicar' to the Archbishop of Paris. In the course of the French Revolution, following the Declaration of the Rights of Man in 1789, Mary Wollstonecraft charged that Rousseau's false dichotomy between the sexes underpinned men's denial to women of the same rights; in her *Vindication of the Rights of Woman* of 1792 she expresses the disappointment of an ardent admirer of his philosophy of education, regarding his comments on women in *Émile* as inconsistent with his complaints, in the *Discourse on Inequality*, against those who confuse civil for savage man. He had rendered women objects of pity, bordering on contempt, she argues, with some apparent justice, by holding the deplorable state into which they had fallen as evidence of their fundamental nature, thus discrediting his mighty sentiments about the human race with trifling remarks about Sophie's delicate feet.

But Wollstonecraft was mistaken to suppose that Rousseau regarded women, on account of their sex, with pity or contempt. On the contrary, he worshipped women and was enchanted by female company, overwhelmed by the delightful conversation of Madame de Luxembourg and by the many kindnesses she showed him at Montmorency, moved to rapturous delight by the prostitute Zulietta in Venice, who nevertheless had scornfully counselled, 'Jacko, give up the ladies, and study mathematics', when

101

his own sexual unease with regard to her uneven breasts frustrated his ardour in an encounter which he describes in his *Confessions* as the most telling incident and revelation of his character throughout his whole life (P i. 320–2, C 300–2). *Émile* was partly conceived out of his love for another Sophie—Sophie d'Houdetot—of a rather different temperament and disposition from the Sophie within his treatise, and in reality a person who, more than all the other women who stirred him, was beyond his reach, except through words. Rousseau typically held women in awe and not derision, supposing their power over men so great that when their nature was debased, as when they became actresses, they were responsible for men's degradation. That had been the main theme of his *Letter to d'Alembert on the Theatre*, he confides to Toussaint-Pierre Lenieps in a letter of 8 November 1758 (L 730). 'Everywhere men are what women make of them', he states there, attributing to the female sex an influence over men's moral lives which in his *Confessions* he ascribes in much the same terms to government. The two sexes must never be separated, he insists, for each depends upon the other—a proposition made plain enough in the *Letter to d'Alembert* itself, where he asserts that 'a home whose mistress is absent is a body without a soul which soon falls into corruption' (A 88).

In *The New Héloïse*, the eighteenth letter of part iii, which turns round Julie's marriage to Wolmar, forms the romantic consummation and centre-piece of the whole novel. Similarly, in *Émile*, the principal function of the passage about Sophie and women is to complete a portrait of the formation of a person's identity from its embryonic isolation to the conjugal bond created by sexual difference. Rousseau's main objective is not to deny Sophie her civil rights or her husband's liberating education. It is, rather, to show the way that the human soul is possessed by love, in the manner of Plato, 'lovers' real philosopher', as Rousseau describes him in *The New Héloïse* (P ii. 223 n.). It is to illustrate to his readers 'how what is physical leads us unwittingly to the moral, and how the sweetest laws of love are born little by little from the coarse union of the sexes' (P iv. 697, E 360), with a fully developed moral being, or *personne morale*, formed out of the complementary attributes of husband and wife, whose cohesion could not be achieved if a woman's role were independently determined. Such union in matrimony, achieved in a domestic setting and prompted from a bodily need and a spiritual *amour-propre*, is entirely unlike an open assembly of citizens in political association, as described in the *Social Contract*; its love binds partners to each other and not the state. 'Forced to combat nature or social institutions, one must choose between making a man or a citizen', Rousseau observes at the beginning of book i of *Émile*, exclaiming, in similar terms, in some fragmentary notes on the subject of public happiness, 'Give man entirely to the state, or leave him entirely to himself, but if you divide his heart you rend it asunder' (P iii. 510, P iv. 248, E 39). Nature's pupil must be plucked from society and left to himself, as if he were an orphan (P iv. 267, E 52). The only book that is specially suited for him, and which for a long time will comprise the whole of his library, is Defoe's *Robinson Crusoe* (P iv. 454–5, E 184).

6 Vagabond Reverie

From internal evidence in *The New Héloïse*, whose events are portrayed as having transpired over a period of more than a dozen years from around 1732, it has long been known that Rousseau invented a fictional protagonist, Saint-Preux, of exactly his own age. To this central figure of his story, as his *Confessions* make plain (P i. 430, C 400–1), he attributes both refined sensibilities and weaknesses of character deliberately drawn from his own nature, and by depicting him as a peripatetic tutor who is deemed by Julie's father to be unworthy of her love on account of being beneath her station, he conveys the impression of a socially outcast romantic hero, doomed to unhappiness, whom readers could readily identify with the text's author. This parallel, together with a number of other superficial resemblances between characters in the novel and figures who populated his world outside it, has invited the suspicion that the most popular of all of Rousseau's works in the eighteenth century was conceived as an illusory representation of events he had actually experienced, an idealization of his autobiography couched in the epistolary form then fashionable for sentimental fiction. It would, however, be more accurate to interpret the novel's occasional *ménage à trois* of Saint-Preux, Julie, and Wolmar, as well as the incidents around which their relationships turn, as expressions of profound longings which, as a matter of fact, Rousseau could barely articulate, still less satisfy, in his own life. Somewhat like his contemporary, Diderot, who often contrived to be at his most intense through a form of displacement which involved speaking his own mind as if he were reporting claims that had been made by others, Rousseau characteristically allowed his vivid imagination to give more concrete form to worlds he could inhabit, and sentiments he could control, only in fantasy.

When he began to contemplate his novel, he remarks that it was largely because his time for love had passed, and all hope for the consummation of a desire which Thérèse was unable to stir in him had withered in his middle age, that he let his imagination draw him into a 'land of chimeras', an empyrean domain inhabited by the most perfect creatures, celestial in both virtue and beauty, and of such faithful reliability as he had never known among his friends here below. It was out of his exalted attraction to such an 'enchanted world' that *The New Héloïse* was born (P i. 427–8, C 398). The novel articulates the secrets of a rapturously ecstatic love which he was later to hope might actually prove the key to Sophie d'Houdetot's heart; but despite the rumours about the nature of his infatuation with her—which were orchestrated by a jealous Madame d'Épinay, and which, with other factors, would soon provoke one of his life's great crises, including his break with Diderot and eventually his estrangement from most of his Parisian friends—Rousseau never conquered Sophie as, in his imagination, he licensed Saint-Preux and Julie to seduce one another. The 'erotic fervour' and 'amorous delirium', which in his *Confessions* he claims were aroused in him by Sophie, came to inspire his composition of two of the most sublime letters of his novel (P i. 438, C 408), one about the hidden orchard of Wolmar and Julie at the retreat she called her *Elyseum*, the other about a day Saint-Preux spent with Julie, in Wolmar's absence, in the waters and along the banks of Lake Geneva (letters 11 and 17 in part iv, respectively). By the winter of 1756, Rousseau was already gripped with love for the figure he had invented in June, doting on both her and her cousin, Claire, like a second Pygmalion, he remarks in his *Confessions* (P ii. 436, C 406). The explosive arrival in his life of Sophie the following year, after an inconsequentially brief meeting earlier, inspired him to invest all of Julie's charms into his new companion as well, soon making him dream only of Sophie herself, as he came to feel his own surging tremors and cascading passion for an object that was now real.

For her part, Sophie, though she was as moved by his intimate presence as he by hers, was not excited in the same way. Their sighs and tears mingled together, as each was intoxicated with love, he reports, Rousseau for her, and she for her absent lover, Saint-Lambert, whom Rousseau had met independently and with whom he was at the same time already beginning to form a friendship. His unreciprocated love for Sophie was thus always accompanied by a third presence, who at once lent poignancy to

Sophie's own need for Rousseau as a confidant, at the same time making it impossible for him, loving her with such profound respect, to seek to possess her. But having had aroused in him by a kind of contagion all the longing which Sophie felt for Saint-Lambert, Rousseau could now consummate a redoubled passion only through the catharsis of its infusion into Julie, a woman he could possess just within his own mind, from which she sprang. Sophie's genuine affection for him, he thus reports, was a poisoned cup of sweetness which he swallowed in long draughts (P iv. 440, C 410). The four months they spent together, in an intimacy of such delicious palpitations as Rousseau states he never experienced with any other woman, were kept within the bounds of duty, whose prescription of self-denial left his own soul in the radiant circumspection of enforced innocence, as he was to inform Sophie herself in a remarkable letter he sent her in October 1757 (L 533), from which this passage of his *Confessions* would later be shaped. Yet so fired were his senses by images of an anticipated kiss that when he would walk along the slopes of Andilly to her home in Eaubonne, three miles from his *Hermitage*, his knees would tremble, his body crumple, and, unable to distract himself and think of something else, he would ejaculate and arrive at the home of a lover he could not win, a spent force purged of the ecstatic transports of his own imagination, only to be roused again at the mere sight of her, by his 'always useless vigour' (P i. 445, C 414–15).

If in his fiction Rousseau could assemble a world purified of such cumbersome anxieties and frustrations, in his other writings he sought equally blissful delights by cleansing moral landscapes of the fractious institutions and tortuous beliefs which he perceived as standing in the way of human self-fulfilment. The fanciful world which he constructed in his *New Héloïse*, at once brittle with dramatic tension but also luminous with unadorned grace, was matched elsewhere by his deconstruction of opaque and oppressive worlds, for which the idealizations of his fiction were a substitute. In his *Letter to d'Alembert on the Theatre*, composed at much the same time as his *New Héloïse* and embracing many overlapping themes, he contrasts the salubrious entertainments of a republic—remarkably like Geneva—where convivial celebrations are held out of doors, under the sky, with the noxious amusements

of the residents of a large city—which rather resembles Paris—
whose scheming and idle people, depraved by sloth, turn instead
for their pleasures to hypocritical distractions performed on a stage.
Let the spectators become an entertainment to themselves, he
remarks, each being granted the role of an engaged actor and not
just a captive witness, loving himself in the others, 'so that all
will be better united' (A 58, 125–6). Shakespeare's melancholic
Jacques in *As You Like It* may have regretted that 'All the world's
a stage', but Jean-Jacques would have rejoiced if only it could be
so.

In his *Discourse on Inequality*, he had earlier formed an image
of savage man no less fancifully cleansed of the impurities and
contaminations of society than was Julie of the worldly imper-
fections of her sex. In *Émile*, he was later to invent an equally
imaginary priest, by way of abstraction from real persons, whose
sublimation of an unmysterious god in Nature would be presented
as a spiritual purge of truly religious belief from all the ceremo-
nial trappings of a profane Church. While 'the real world has its
limits, the world of imagination is infinite', Rousseau remarks in
book ii of *Émile*, adding in book iv, in reply to those of his readers
who supposed he only inhabited a world of fantasy, that he sees
them 'always in the land of prejudice' (P iv. 305, 549; E 81, 253).
Most of his major writings, fiction and non-fiction alike, bear
witness to James Boswell's remark, in a letter of 15 October 1766
to Alexandre Deleyre, that he had ideas which were 'completely
visionary, and unsuitable for a man in his position' (L 5477). That
'involuntary excitement', 'devouring ardour', or 'sublime frenzy',
that 'sacred fire', 'noble delirium', or 'saintly enthusiasm', of which
he speaks in just a single paragraph of the fourth of his *Moral
Letters* to Sophie (P iv. 1101), sparks the disengagement of our
faculties from their terrestrial ties. While our reason crawls, our
spirit soars, he observes. No other eighteenth-century writer so
inspired the Romantic movement which arose, most predominantly
in Germany and England, at the dusk of the age of Enlightenment,
by the intensity of his feelings, the rapture of his dreams, and the
spontaneity of his imagination.

Even before it had absorbed his attention in the principal works
by which he is now best remembered, Rousseau's vagabond reverie drew him most fruitfully in the direction of music, a subject

for which he had been born, he insists in both his *Confessions* and *Dialogues* (P i. 181, 872; C 175). In his reflections on the inappropriateness of the French language to musical articulation, and in his objections to Rameau's claims about the predominance of harmony over melody, he conceived music to have once been the ebullient form taken by men's natural language, unmannered and unsophisticated, as enchanted in its enunciation as Julie's loveliness appeared to his mind's eye. Sung with conviction in inflected phrases, and freed of orchestral ornamentation and operatic recitative, a clear vocal line of music was in some respects the most populist of all the fanciful images that Rousseau evoked of mankind's archaic means of self-expression, the lost primeval language of unsubjugated speech. Shorn of the pretence that the dominant and subdominant modes of the Western scale were inherent in every form of music, its original nature could be traced in his philosophy to its fundamentally poetic roots, and its progressive transformations from an ancient art into a modern science could be reconstructed in the manner of his treatment of the self-domestication of mankind in other ways.

But the origins of modern and Western music were not so remote as those of inequality, and Rousseau was accordingly able to assess the course of its development in far less speculative terms. Already in his contributions to the *Encyclopédie*, he had shown a genuine command of the history of music and of musical genres, and particularly of contemporary musical theory, pursuing themes in his articles 'Accompaniment', 'Dissonance', and 'Fundamental Bass' which largely elaborated Rameau's own views on harmonic modulation and on the overtone resonances of a single note, prompting Diderot and d'Alembert to object, in the *Encyclopédie*'s sixth volume, that Rameau had ungraciously maligned a man who had in fact been largely faithful to his principles. Even in the enlarged versions of those articles that he incorporated in his *Dictionary of Music*, Rousseau still acknowledges a profound debt to Rameau's *Theory of Harmony*, which had been published in 1722. But to comply with Diderot's initial deadline, he had produced his original articles in only three months and had long sought an opportunity to return to and expand them, to pursue his differences with Rameau where they arose, and to elaborate themes which he had been unable to consider earlier.

The *Dictionary of Music* was conceived as a work of reference, and it did not excite him to flights of fancy as did most of the other projects to which he turned at *The Hermitage*, after leaving Paris. For this reason, as he remarks in his *Confessions*, he put it aside when taking the daily walks which spawned his reveries, and, exceptionally, he worked out his ideas for it indoors, seated, when it rained (P iv. 410, C 382). It is, nevertheless, one of his major works, comprehensive in its treatment of historical, technical, and theoretical subjects, not only making the complexities of Rameau's doctrines more intelligible to lay readers, as d'Alembert had attempted to do as well, but also providing thoroughly revised and more substantial commentaries on ancient, medieval, and modern practices of notation in his article on 'Notes'; a fresh essay on the history of lyrical drama (which in the *Encyclopédie* had instead been allocated to Grimm, under the heading of 'Lyrical Poem') in his article on 'Opera'; and an analysis of the musical theory of Tartini in his article on 'System'. Charles Burney, who had earlier translated the libretto of Rousseau's opera *Le Devin du village* or *Village Soothsayer* into English, as *The Cunning-Man*, spoke in his own *General History of Music* in defence of Rousseau against the critics of both his *Letter on French Music* and his *Dictionary of Music*, while Rousseau himself, who had sketched a decidedly mixed assessment of the opera *Alceste*, by Gluck (1767), is reported to have suggested that Gluck's remarkable *Iphigenia in Aulis* (1774), with a French libretto, perhaps finally belied his contention that it was impossible to write music with French lyrics.

Even in his *Dictionary of Music*, however, he retained and lent additional impetus to ideas which had first fired his imagination in the late 1740s and early 1750s. In a new article on 'Plainsong', he observes that it was when Christians began to form churches and to sing psalms and hymns that the spirited music of antiquity lost all its energy. From both Scripture and classical sources, most particularly the Pythagoreans, he adds in his article on 'Music'—repeating remarks he had made in the *Encyclopédie* and recalling Plato's *Laws*—we know that both divine and human law, as well as exhortations to virtue, were once sung in verse by choirs, there being no more effective way to teach men the love of virtue. Everything that can be elicited in the imagination stems from the power of poetry from which music once sprang, he claims in his articles on both 'Imitation' and 'Opera', in each case showing his lack of appreciation and poor discernment of the emotive powers of painting, by contrast with his sensitivity to music—perhaps the most striking difference between his aesthetic judgement and that of Diderot. Unlike painting, which inspires only our sense of sight, Rousseau contends, music transports the eye inside the ear, and depicts even objects which are invisible, like night, sleep, solitude, and silence, noise sometimes producing the effect of perfect tranquillity and silence the effect of noise, as persons who fall asleep at a monotonous lecture and wake up the minute it stops know only too well. Rousseau's interest in music was sustained throughout his life, not least because, having resolved around 1750 to copy music by the sheet so that he might have some regular and independent income, he drew from that occupation, almost until his end, one of the few means of support on which he could count as a writer determined to refuse all favours or pensions, thus avoiding debts that might imperil his freedom. In the greatly distracted state in which he finally fled from England in the spring of 1767, he was nevertheless prevailed upon, by Hume, to accept just such a gift from the eventually far more demented King George III, and in due course, against his principles, he received the sum of £50 for nothing.

Once again in France, over the next three years, Rousseau became, both in his own mind and in fact, an itinerant hostage to fortune, travelling under a cloak of anonymity as Monsieur 'Renou', accompanied by his housekeeper, said to be his sister. The Enlightenment's most forthright lover of truth, who had for so long devoted his energies to unmasking hypocrisy, was now in disguise himself, flitting from Trye, on the border of Normandy, to Bourgoin and Monquin in Dauphiné, to Lyons and finally Paris, along the way visiting the grave of Madame de Warens in Chambéry and soon afterwards marrying Thérèse, in meanderings made all the more furtive by his principal patron of that time, the Prince de Conti—who really *was* a warder masquerading as a protector— while Rousseau was ignored by the authorities he sought to evade, because they judged him more absurd than dangerous. It was especially in this period that he turned his mind to the subject of botany, the great passion of his declining years. In Môtiers, after his flight from Montmorency, he had already become acquainted with the distinguished botanist, Jean-Antoine d'Ivernois and had there made lengthy botanical excursions into the surrounding countryside with the Hungarian pseudo-baron Ignaz de Sauttersheim, the Pierre Loti of his age, whose life was more fictitious than all the fantasies of *The New Héloïse*. In Staffordshire, Rousseau had gathered ferns and mosses. But it was in the late 1760s, either alone or with a variety of companions, in the hinterland of Trye, Lyons, Grenoble, Bourgoin, and Monquin, that he came to devote most of his time to the study of plants, arousing occasional suspicions that he was a sorcerer.

On his return to Paris in the summer of 1770, he was to resume his profession of transcribing music each morning, and in the afternoons would botanize and herborize in the course of long strolls which he took out of the city. On various dates between 1771 and 1773, he drafted eight long letters on botanical themes to Madame Madeleine-Catherine Delessert, to whom he had warmed after an earlier meeting in Lyons, and who wished to excite her four-year-old daughter's natural curiosity by encouraging her to take an interest in plants. These letters, followed over the next four years by sixteen others on similar themes to various correspondents (all published with Rousseau's complete works in 1782), were to excite the interest of Thomas Martyn, a professor of botany at Cambridge who held his chair for sixty-three years and for at least part of that time used his own translation of them in his courses; and they were also taken up by the painter Pierre Joseph Redouté, who illustrated them for a luxurious edition of Rousseau's botanical writings published early in the nineteenth century. Around this time, Rousseau also compiled, but never completed, a dictionary of botanical terms. He continued as well to assemble the herbaria, on which he had already laboured even earlier, and of which a few survive, although the largest collection, forming eleven volumes, perished with Berlin's botanical museum in the Second World War.

Rousseau's acquired interest in botany seems a sensible choice of vocation for a man whose faculties were most alive while he was walking, his mind only working with his legs, as he remarks in his *Confessions* (P i. 410, C 382). Here, at last, Nature's ageing child could commune directly with the great spectacle of Creation, before which he had always stood in awe—like a more youthful Émile, within reach of contentment, his power and will in equilibrium. Here was a subject whose lively colours and fragrances could fill his imagination, an Arcadian paradise of vegetable love, such as had equally seduced the poet Andrew Marvell a century earlier. In the Second Walk of his *Reveries*, he recalls the sweet pleasure he had felt in seeing and enumerating the plants still in flower in the meadows, between Ménilmontant and Charonne near Paris, which are now partly filled by the Père Lachaise Cemetery (P i. 1003–4, R 36–8). In the Seventh Walk, devoted largely to the trees and vegetation which are 'the clothing of the earth', he savours the memory of a mountain gorge, where he had found coral-wort and cyclamen, and heard the cry of the horned owl and eagle, in a corner of the earth so deeply hidden that, when he had sat down on pillows of *lycopodium*, he dreamt he had stumbled upon the wildest and most remote refuge of the universe, having uncovered, like a second, lone, Columbus, a sanctuary from which his persecutors would never seek him out (P i. 1062, 1070–1; R 108, 117–18). Here, now recollected as a botanical expedition he had made near Môtiers around 1764, was Rousseau's own *Elyseum*, originally inspired in the spring of 1757 by the arrival in his life of Sophie d'Houdetot, and described, in *The New Héloïse*, in remarkably similar terms, as Julie's secret orchard, 'the wildest, the most solitary, corner of Nature' (P ii. 471). His love for Sophie had passed from one captivating heart of darkness to another, in retrodiction of his own life by way of imitating his own art. From sensual arousal, to fiction, to remembrance of now transported images, Rousseau—in this as in so many other respects the Proust of the eighteenth century—could make his botany and reverie resonate in one voice.

He had not always been so well disposed to the study of plants. If only he had succumbed to the temptation to follow Claude Anet, the young herbalist Madame de Warens had employed at Chambéry, and with whom he was to share her love, he might have become a great botanist himself, he suggests. But, ignorant of its charms, he had let himself be swayed by popular prejudice that it was a science like chemistry or anatomy, connected with medicine or pharmacology and fit only for apothecaries, he claims in his *Confessions*, his *Reveries*, and even the introduction to his dictionary of botanical terms (P i. 180–1, 1063–4; P iv. 1201; C 175; R 109–10). Nothing could be further from the truth, he had later learned. And in what other science could he have passed his time? How could he have chased after animals, only in order to subdue them by force if he could catch them and then, in order to understand how they run, dissect them? If too weak, he could no doubt have impaled butterflies instead; if too slow, he could have fallen back on snails and worms; yet all those stinking corpses, dreadful skeletons, and pestilential vapours had not been for him. Nor had he wished, with the aid of instruments and machines, to study the stars. But bright flowers, cool shades, streams, woods, meadows, and green glades had purified his imagination, he remarks in the Seventh Walk of his *Reveries*. Plants had been placed within man's reach by Nature Herself, springing up beneath the feet of a person whose mind had already settled there (P i. 1068–9, R 114–15).

Of course the meticulous and disciplined study of plants must not be confused with the agreeable sensations which inspire it, Rousseau admits in his dictionary (P iv. 1220–1). Botany, as he understood it, was essentially a taxonomic science which, if it did not necessarily dissect its objects of scrutiny, nevertheless sought to classify them and establish the purpose of their internal organization, he observes in his *Reveries*. In both his dictionary and his botanical letters he accordingly addresses his attention to the parts of fruits and flowers—to the pistils, calyces, and panicles of plants—whose identity and function he learnt from several authorities, especially the *Systema naturae*, *Philosophia botanica*, and *Regnum vegetabile* of Linnaeus, the pre-eminent botanist of the eighteenth century, to whom he once corresponded, as well as an essay by one of Linnaeus's principal editors, Johann Anders Murray. Rousseau sometimes confused one plant's or organ's description with another's, and he occasionally misunderstood the principles he borrowed. Perhaps because he preferred the study of plants to that of animals, moreover, it never occurred to him that they might also be investigated in terms of their natural or artificially bred history, along such lines as were pursued by Buffon in his commentaries on the degeneration of species, which had so impressed him in his account of mankind's development in the *Discourse on Inequality*. For botanical investigations, if not for the science of human nature, his model was Linnaeus rather than

Buffon. His inspiration, nevertheless, was that of a man whose mind and sensibilities were most active when he was alone, out of doors, tramping in celebration of Nature. Botany, he remarks in his *Reveries* (P i. 1069, R 115), is the ideal subject of study for the idle and unoccupied solitary man.

It was not, however, the only field to which Rousseau turned in his solitude, at once enforced upon him by his estrangement from society, and at the same time relished on account of the freedom it afforded his flights of fancy. There remained one other subject of his final years, whose appeal he felt even more powerfully, because it was inescapable and because reflection upon it had always supplied him with the critical lens through which he perused everything else—that is, himself. Rousseau claims that it was around 1760 that he first contemplated an autobiography, and by 1765, with all the major works on which he had embarked almost a decade earlier at *The Hermitage* either in print or ready for press or abandoned, he turned to his *Confessions* in earnest and assembled them principally from his voluminous correspondence, including copies or drafts of his own letters which he had kept. Knowing his ways, his eloquence, and his bias, some of his former friends, who were certain they would be maligned by him, took the precaution of maligning him, either first or as well, none more than Madame d'Épinay, who, in return for her solicitude and affection after providing him with his first refuge, had been unjustly accused by him of duplicity and treachery. Her original indiscretions, revolving around Rousseau's infatuation with Sophie, had never warranted his venomous charges against her, but she was to repay his discourtesy and insults with interest. Joined by Diderot, she requested and obtained official prohibition of Rousseau's public readings from the manuscript of his *Confessions* after his return to Paris, and with the assistance of Grimm and Diderot, as her own surviving papers make plain, she reassembled and even rewrote the letters she exchanged with Rousseau at the time of their break, so as to make him appear perfidious throughout the whole period of their relationship, in the account she offers in her pseudo-memoirs, published posthumously in 1818, known as the *Story of Madame de Montbrillant*. In part endeavouring to protect themselves from his scurrilous imputations, but also out of genuine and even mounting contempt for a man whose outrageous vanity seemed to them boundless, Rousseau's enemies embarked on a variety of stratagems to discredit him, which of course always had the effect of confirming, not only his original mistrust of their character, but also his suspicions of a conspiracy to defame him. In the history of Western civilization, no major figure has ever surpassed Rousseau in his ability to confuse mere imprudence with sinister intent, leading to dreadfully escalating consequences thereafter.

In *Rousseau, Judge of Jean-Jacques*, better known by its subtitle, *Dialogues*, drafted mainly between 1772 and 1774, he allows free rein to his by now truly formidable paranoia. He is a bear who must be kept in chains so as not to eat the peasants, Rousseau has an interlocutor called 'the Frenchman' say about himself (P i. 716). Since his poisonous pen is so dreaded, how can gentlemen in such apprehension of this monstrous misanthrope conspire so assiduously to hound him (P i. 725)? The *Dialogues* were to be published in 1780 in Lichfield, Samuel Johnson's birthplace. More frenetically conceived on the wilder side of reason than any of his other works, they form a text which Rousseau tried to transmit to mankind by way of disencumbrance, seeking to leave it in the hands of Providence through placing it on the altar of Notre Dame, only to find that the choir had been locked, his appeal to the world thereby silenced in still-birth, even escape from himself denied him. In recent years it has attracted the attention of Michel Foucault in particular, who introduced it in a modern edition. But it is infrequently read today, and still more seldom read without pain.

Rousseau's last major work, the *Reveries*, begun in 1776 and unfinished at the time of his death, is of a radically different character. Its opening passage, among the most poignant he ever penned, captures the tribulations of a life now purged of its anxieties and is presented as if it were the work's last lines, recalling all that had gone before: 'So now I am alone in the world, with no brother, neighbour, or friend, nor any company left me but my own. The most sociable and loving of men has with unanimous accord been cast out by all the rest' (P i. 995, R 27). In a series of Ten Walks, or promenades, which conclude with a regression to his beloved *maman* and the idyllic peace he savoured with her in his youth, Rousseau rehearses many themes about his estrangement from society drawn from his other writings—depicting the perambulating mind of an old man, with all his faculties now restored, forever spiralling backwards. The Seventh, Ninth, and, above all, Fifth of these walks constitute the work's spiritual centre—the Seventh revealing the wilderness of his botanical *Elyseum*, the Ninth forming his lament on the inconstancy of happiness, and the Fifth recalling a watery bliss on an island sanctuary—comprising, in effect, the pastoral, heroic, and choral symphonies of Rousseau's reverie. In the Ninth Walk, he attempts to excuse the abandonment of his children and describes the juvenile impetuosity of his character, as well as the irresistible joy he feels at the mere sight of happy faces. But throughout the walk, he adopts a tone of sombre resignation at his fate, insisting that all our plans for happiness are just fantasy, there being no permanent way to secure contentment.

In the Fifth Walk, he appears to put forward similar sentiments with more intense conviction, stating that 'everything is in constant flux on this earth', our affections, being attached to things outside us, inevitably changing and passing away with their objects, our worldly joys but fleeting creatures of a moment (P i. 1046, R 88). Yet in the same walk, recollecting his flight from Môtiers in September 1765, when he had found refuge on the Island of Saint-Pierre in the middle of the Lake of Bienne, he evokes images of a sheltered haven so beautiful that he could have written about every blade of grass in the meadows and every lichen covering the rocks, where he had spent afternoons exploring the sallows, persicarias, and shrubs of all kinds, or had lain outstretched in a boat, drifting wherever the waters would take him, 'plunged in a thousand indistinct and yet delightful reveries'— a sanctum of such exquisite happiness that he would have been content to live there all his life, 'without a moment's desire for any other state' (P i. 1042–4, R 83–5). Just as his Seventh Walk displaces Julie's *Elyseum* to a past he now suggests had been his own, so does his Fifth Walk thus transport a fictional day's outing on the banks of Lake Geneva—which Saint-Preux had likewise described in strikingly similar detail as 'the day when he had experienced the most vivid emotions of his entire life' (P ii. 521)— to an island retreat of rampant beauty, cut off by Nature Herself from the manufactured turmoil of contemporary civilization. In escaping from the mundane crises of his life through reverie, Rousseau could dissolve all difference between recollection and invention. Transported by his own imagination, and carried with it into a celestial domain of pure bliss such as he describes in his third letter to Malesherbes, he could inhabit alternative worlds of perfect serenity uniquely fit for him.

In his major writings, and the various disciplines they address, he sought to give substance to such ideals by expunging all the institutions which obstructed their fulfilment, so that through a process of sublime negativity he could illuminate realms of unprosaic speech and unembellished music, of human nature without society, an education without teachers, a city without theatres, a state without rulers, a divine presence without a church. By way of such regressions, Rousseau not only posited diverse visions of men's self-realization in a condition of unfettered freedom. He also disengaged himself more dramatically from his own age of Enlightenment, appearing less circumscribed by the presuppositions and conventions of its discourses than any other major thinker of his day. In some of its registers, his intransigently critical voice still speaks with undiminished vigour more than two hundred years after his death. Modern and post-modern philosophers and writers alike often owe a considerable debt to his works which they are sometimes loath to acknowledge, and more often still they espouse views to which, in earlier formulations, he had already objected himself. In Rousseau's pursuit of a language of pure sincerity, in his ideal of truly communicative agents, engaged by their speech acts, taking full part in the articulation of public choice, can be found anticipations of the political philosophy of Jürgen Habermas, for instance. In his perception of the suffocating, mutilating, and dehumanizing tyrannies of modern commercial society, portrayed as if it were the panopticon of a Procrustean rather than Promethean monster assembled by a still-to-be-born Dr Frankenstein masquerading as Bentham, he also points some of the way towards Foucault. Yet, as distinct from most post-modernist thinkers and their critics alike, Rousseau was to find refuge and achieve tranquillity, even while buffeted in a personal and political world of continual turbulence. From both introspection and good grace, the most formidable eighteenth-century critic of the trappings of civilization, and the most vivid illustrator of the textures of its despair and discontent, believed all his life, no less than did Anne Frank at the darkest moment of modern history, that human nature was still fundamentally good at heart.

Further Reading

SVEC: *Studies on Voltaire and the Eighteenth Century*

General Collections, Commentaries, and Biographies

Indispensable to Rousseau scholarship today are two major publishing ventures of the past thirty-five years, the Pléiade edition of his *Œuvres complètes*, compiled by B. Gagnebin, M. Raymond, and others (Paris, 1959–), and the Voltaire Foundation edition of his *Correspondance complète*, by R. A. Leigh (Geneva and Oxford, 1965–). Each is drawn from the original manuscripts and is richly documented with editorial notes, illustrating Rousseau's sources and parallel passages across his writings. As of November 1993, the long-awaited fifth volume of the Pléiade *Œuvres complètes*, including his musical writings, is still not in print, but two particularly fine editions of the *Essai sur l'origine des langues* are available, one by Charles Porset (2nd edn., Bordeaux, 1970), the other by Jean Starobinski (Paris, 1990). Of Rousseau's principal works already incorporated in the Pléiade edition, perhaps only the *Discours sur les sciences et les arts* is presented with more compelling command of its sources elsewhere, by George Havens (New York, 1946). The extensively annotated translation of Rousseau's *Collected Writings* (Hanover, NH, 1990–) currently in progress under the general supervision of Roger Masters and Christopher Kelly, when finished, should provide the best, and in several instances the first, editions of his works for English readers. Of the major writings, including the *Discours sur l'inégalité*, the *Contrat social*, the *Confessions*, and the *Rêveries*, there are numerous, often fine, translations into English available already, or about to become available, including those contained in the series of Texts in the History of Political Thought (Cambridge University Press) and the World's Classics series (Oxford University Press). Leigh's edition of the *Correspondance complète*, currently in fifty volumes and awaiting only its several tomes of indexes, is one of the most remarkable works of modern scholarship in any field—its annotation majestic, its powers of resuscitating Rousseau's world, and even the spontaneity and refinement of the composition of his ideas, unsurpassed.

This correspondence, and Rousseau's own *Confessions*, have helped make it possible for Maurice Cranston to produce two volumes thus far of the finest biography of Rousseau in any language (London, 1983, 1991), although Jean Guéhenno's *Jean-Jacques Rousseau* (Eng. trans., 2 vols., London,

1966) and Lester Crocker's *Jean-Jacques Rousseau* (2 vols., New York, 1968, 1973) also have merit. Ronald Grimsley's *Jean-Jacques Rousseau: A Study of Self-Awareness* (2nd edn., Cardiff, 1969) offers a particularly sensitive treatment of the development of Rousseau's personality through his writings, while Kelly's *Rousseau's Exemplary Life: The 'Confessions' as Political Philosophy* (Ithaca, NY, 1987) interprets the autobiography in the light of his principles.

Among English-language commentaries of his thought in different genres, perhaps Ernst Cassirer's *The Question of Jean-Jacques Rousseau* (2nd edn., New Haven, Conn., 1989), Judith Shklar's *Men and Citizens: A Study of Rousseau's Social Theory* (2nd edn., Cambridge, 1985), and C. W. Hendel's more comprehensive *Jean-Jacques Rousseau: Moralist* (2nd edn., Indianapolis, 1962) excel, Hendel's work in particular being among the most subtly detailed accounts of Rousseau's philosophy in any language. In French, the most remarkable treatments of his thought are probably Bronisław Baczko's *Rousseau: Solitude et communauté*, originally published in Polish (Paris 1974), Pierre Burgelin's *La Philosophie de l'existence de J.-J. Rousseau* (2nd edn., Paris, 1973), and Starobinski's classic study, dating from 1957, now available in English, *Jean-Jacques Rousseau: Transparency and Obstruction* (Chicago, 1988), which is dazzling in its images of Rousseau's inner experience and metaphors of opaque reflection.

John Hope Mason, in *The Indispensable Rousseau* (London, 1979), offers English readers a skilful single-volume commentary, interwoven with selections from almost all of Rousseau's major writings, while N. J. H. Dent, in *A Rousseau Dictionary* (Oxford, 1992), provides a well-conceived thematic treatment of Rousseau's works, with useful pointers in each case to the pertinent secondary literature. The Société Jean-Jacques Rousseau, based in Geneva, has since 1905 produced a journal of remarkable erudition, the *Annales*, and for those who find that they can never have enough of Rousseau, there is a computer-generated *Collection des index et concordances* of his writings still in progress (Geneva and Paris, 1977–), under the general supervision of Michel Launay and dedicated colleagues at the University of Nice and elsewhere.

Studies of Rousseau's Political and Social Thought

Still the most authoritative interpretation of Rousseau's political works in their historical context is Robert Derathé's *Rousseau et la science politique de son temps* (2nd edn., Paris, 1970), which offers a richly detailed account of the jurisprudential background to his philosophy. Masters, in *The Political Philosophy of Rousseau* (Princeton, NJ, 1968), provides one of the best-documented and most closely argued readings of Rousseau's political and educational writings, in so far as they form parts of a systematic doctrine which unfolds from the first *Discours*, while in *Jean-Jacques Rousseau: Écrivain politique (1712–1762)* (Cannes and Grenoble, 1971), Launay, writing from an essentially Marxian perspective, also shows a profound command of major and minor texts alike.

Among significant treatments of the *Discours sur les sciences et les arts*, either independently or in connection with Rousseau's other writings which spring most immediately from it, are Mario Einaudi's *The Early Rousseau* (Ithaca, NY, 1967); Victor Gourevitch's 'Rousseau on the Arts and Sciences', *Journal of Philosophy*, 69 (1972); Havens's 'The Road to Rousseau's *Discours sur l'inégalité*', *Diderot Studies*, 3 (1961); and Hope Mason's 'Reading Rousseau's First Discourse', *SVEC* 249 (1987). The *Discours sur l'inégalité*, central as it is to Rousseau's political theory, has in recent years received perhaps even closer scholarly attention for its philosophy of history, for instance in Asher Horowitz's *Rousseau: Nature and History* (Toronto, 1986), and above all for its philosophical or historical anthropology, most notably in Michèle Duchet's *Anthropologie et histoire au siècle des lumières* (Paris, 1971); Victor Goldschmidt's *Anthropologie et politique: Les principes du système de Rousseau* (Paris, 1974); and Arthur M. Melzer's *The Natural Goodness of Man: On the System of Rousseau's Thought* (Chicago, 1990). I have attempted to deal with the several contexts of Rousseau's argument at some length in my *Rousseau's 'Discours sur l'inégalité' and its Sources*, at long last in press, as a volume of *SVEC*. Differing perspectives on his account of mankind's savage nature, and on his claims about apes and orang-utans, can be found in Arthur O. Lovejoy, 'Rousseau's Supposed Primitivism', in Lovejoy, *Essays on the History of Ideas* (Baltimore, 1948); Gourevitch, 'Rousseau's Pure State of Nature', *Interpretation*, 16 (1988); Francis Moran III, 'Natural Man in the *Second Discourse*', *Journal of the History of Ideas*, 54 (1993); and my 'Perfectible Apes in Decadent Cultures: Rousseau's Anthropology Revisited', *Daedalus*, 107 (1978). Jacques Derrida's *De la grammatologie* (Paris, 1967) embraces one of the subtlest treatments available of the *Essai sur l'origine des langues*.

Notable discussions of the argument of the *Contrat social* range from Andrew Levine's sympathetic Kantian perspective in *The Politics of Autonomy* (Amherst, Mass., 1976), passing through John W. Chapman's balanced *Rousseau—Totalitarian or Liberal?* (New York, 1956), Zev Trachtenberg's discriminating *Making Citizens: Rousseau's Political Theory of Culture* (New York, 1993), and John Plamenatz's judicious *Man and Society*, vol. ii (2nd edn., London, 1992). Patrick Riley's *Will and Political Legitimacy: A Critical Exposition of Social Contract Theory in Hobbes, Locke, Rousseau, Kant and Hegel* (Cambridge, Mass., 1982) offers an especially salient treatment of Rousseau's conception of the general will as part of a tradition of political voluntarism, while Richard Fralin's *Rousseau and Representation* (New York, 1978), attempts to bring the heady political principles of Rousseau down to earth in their application to actual states. By contrast, Baczko's *Lumières de l'utopie* (Paris, 1978) raises them skywards again in its commentary on *The Government of Poland*; as does James Miller's *Rousseau: Dreamer of Democracy* (New Haven, Conn., 1984), which identifies Rousseau's alpine visions of Genevan democracy with his naturalistic reverie; and Paule-Monique Vernes's *La Ville, la fête, la démocratie: Rousseau et les illusions de la communauté* (Paris, 1978), which locates images of fraternal assembly throughout his political writings in general, including the *Lettre à d'Alembert sur les spectacles*. Among the more striking commentaries on the political significance of theatre in that work is Patrick Coleman's *Rousseau's Political Imagination: Rule and Representation in the 'Lettre à d'Alembert'* (Geneva, 1984).

On Rousseau's influence upon the course of the French Revolution, the documents and notes of volumes 46 to 49 of the Leigh edition of the *Correspondance complète* (which ends not with the death of Rousseau but with that of Thérèse Levasseur in 1801) provide at least as much illumination as any of the separate works, among which the fullest treatment can be found in Roger Barny's *L'Éclatement révolutionnaire du rousseauisme* (Paris, 1988), with more broadly sketched perspectives in Carol Blum's *Rousseau and the Republic of Virtue: The Language of Politics in the French Revolution* (Ithaca, NY, 1986) and Joan McDonald's *Rousseau and the French Revolution: 1762–1791* (London, 1965).

Assessments of his other Writings, Intellectual Relationships, and Sources

On Rousseau's philosophy of education in *Émile*, Dent's treatment of *amour-propre* in that work in *Rousseau: An Introduction to his Psychological, Social and Political Theory* (Oxford, 1988) is compelling, while Peter D. Jimack's *Genèse et la rédaction de l''Émile'* in *SVEC* 13 (1960) is specially informative on the stages of *Émile*'s composition. Pierre-Maurice Masson, the greatest Rousseau scholar of his day, remains a towering presence in his treatment of Rousseau's Christian and natural theology in *La Religion de Rousseau* (3 vols., Paris, 1916), although Ronald Grimsley's more modest *Rousseau and the Religious Quest* (Oxford, 1968) is also helpful. On Rousseau's ideas of sexuality, Allan Bloom's *Love and Friendship* (New York, 1993) addresses the miraculous metamorphosis of sex into love by way of the imagination, while Joel Schwartz's *The Sexual Politics of Rousseau* (Chicago, 1984) identifies two distinct lines of argument about sexual difference in his writings, a subject further pursued from a critical theorist's perspective by Judith Still in *Justice and Difference in the Works of Rousseau* (Cambridge, 1993). Henri Guillemin, in *Un homme, deux ombres (Jean-Jacques—Julie—Sophie)* (Geneva, 1943), offers a lyrical account of Rousseau's passion for Sophie d'Houdetot.

Jean-Louis Lecercle provides a particularly sensitive reading of *La Nouvelle Héloïse* in *Rousseau et l'art du roman* (Paris, 1969), and the novel is also subjected to close analysis by Lionel Gossman, in 'The Worlds of *La Nouvelle Héloïse*', *SVEC* 41 (1966), and by James F. Jones, in *La Nouvelle Héloïse: Rousseau and Utopia* (Geneva, 1977). Jones, in turn, offers a commentary on Rousseau's most distressed work, described as particularly inspired by his stay in England, in *Rousseau's 'Dialogues': An Interpretive Essay* (Geneva, 1991). Françoise Barguillet, in *Rousseau ou l'illusion passionnée: Les rêveries du promeneur solitaire* (Paris, 1991), and Marc Eigeldinger, in *Jean-Jacques Rousseau et la realité de l'imaginaire* (Neuchâtel, 1962), address mainly the overarching form and specific imagery, respectively, of Rousseau's last major work, the *Rêveries*, while Marcel Raymond, in *Jean-Jacques Rousseau: La quête de soi et la rêverie* (Paris 1986), pursues its illuminations into Rousseau's character.

Despite a rapidly growing number of treatments of particular themes within and around his philosophy of music, there is still much scope for original research in this field, and room for a major study of Rousseau's ideas on music as a whole, to supplant Albert Jansen's formidable *Rousseau als Musiker* (Berlin, 1884), and enlarge upon Samuel Baud-Bovy's musicologically well informed but less theoretically focused *Jean-Jacques Rousseau et la musique* (Neuchâtel, 1988). Philip Robinson's *Jean-Jacques Rousseau's Doctrine of the Arts* (Berne, 1984) is particularly helpful on the *Dictionnaire de musique* and certain musical themes throughout Rousseau's writings in general, which are also treated at some length in the fourth chapter and appendix of my *Rousseau on Society, Politics, Music and Language: An Historical Interpretation of his Early Writings* (New York, 1987). On the subject of botany, excellent as is the commentary of Gagnebin in his edition of Rousseau's *Lettres sur la botanique* (Paris, 1962), Jansen's *Rousseau als Botaniker* (Berlin, 1885), of which some fragments have been translated into English by Sir Gavin de Beer in 'Jean-Jacques Rousseau: Botanist', *Annals of Science*, 10 (1954), remains the touchstone for all serious students. The most remarkable treatments of Rousseau's Swiss inheritance, preoccupations, and anxieties are probably to be found in Frédéric Eigeldinger's *'Des pierres dans mon jardin': Les années neuchâteloises de J. J. Rousseau et la crise de 1765* (Geneva, 1992); François Jost's *Jean-Jacques Rousseau Suisse: Étude sur sa personnalité et sa pensée* (2 vols., Fribourg, 1961); and John S. Spink's *Jean-Jacques Rousseau et Genève* (Paris, 1934).

Further Reading

For Rousseau's debt to Machiavelli, Maurizio Virolli's *Jean-Jacques Rousseau and the 'Well-ordered Society'* (Cambridge, 1988) is helpful, as is the treatment of his confrontation of Hobbes in Howard Cell's and James MacAdam's *Rousseau's Response to Hobbes* (Berne, 1988). I have assessed his appreciation of Pufendorf in my 'Rousseau's Pufendorf: Natural Law and the Foundations of Commercial Society', *History of Political Thought*, 15 (1994). Henri Gouhier's *Rousseau et Voltaire: Portraits dans deux miroirs* (Paris, 1983) is masterful in its unravelling of the differences between the two principal antagonists of the age of Enlightenment, while still unsurpassed as a treatment of Rousseau's early intellectual development against the background of the *Encyclopédie* is René Hubert's *Rousseau et l''Encyclopédie': Essai sur la formation des idées politiques de Rousseau (1742–56)* (Paris, 1928), a theme I have pursued specifically with reference to Diderot in 'The Influence of Diderot on the Political Theory of Rousseau: Two Aspects of a Relationship', *SVEC* 132 (1975).

On Rousseauism in France at the end of the eighteenth century, Jean Roussel's *Rousseau en France après la Révolution, 1795–1830* (Paris, 1972) provides the most comprehensive treatment; as, with respect to Germany, does Jacques Mounier's *La Fortune des écrits de Rousseau dans les pays de langue allemande de 1782 à 1813* (Paris, 1980); with regard to Italy, Silvia Rota Ghibaudi's *La fortuna di Rousseau in Italia (1750–1815)* (Turin, 1961); and, in English thought, Henri Roddier's *J.-J. Rousseau en Angleterre au XVIIIᵉ siècle* (Paris, 1950) and Jacques Voisine's *Rousseau en Angleterre à l'époque romantique* (Paris, 1956). Guillemin's *'Cette affaire infernale': L'affaire J. J. Rousseau–David Hume, 1766* (4th edn., Paris, 1942) offers a lively reading of Rousseau's year of torment in the hands of a man who meant him well. For anticipations of Kant in Rousseau's philosophy, the classic text remains Cassirer's *Rousseau, Kant and Goethe*, first published in 1945 (New York, 1963).

Index

Index

Index

Index

Index